STANDING ON THE SIDELINES

ROGER J SIMMONDS

The right of Roger Simmonds to be identified as the
Author of the Work has been asserted by him in accordance
with the Copyright, Designs
and Patents Act 1988.

Some names and identifying details have been
changed to protect the privacy of individuals.

Copyright © Roger Simmonds 2016

Edited by Shaun Russell,
Will Rees and Hayley Cox

Cover by Shaun Russell

ISBN: 978-0-9933221-9-8

Published by
Candy Jar Books
Mackintosh House
136 Newport Road, Cardiff, CF24 1DJ
www.candyjarbooks.co.uk

All rights reserved.
No part of this publication may be reproduced, stored in a
retrieval system, or transmitted at any time or by any means,
electronic, mechanical, photocopying, recording or otherwise
without the prior permission of the copyright holder. This
book is sold subject to the condition that it shall not by way
of trade or otherwise be circulated without the publisher's
prior consent in any form of binding or cover
other than that in which it is published.

I would like to thank my wife Kenet for standing by me for the last thirty three years and for encouraging me to take up new challenges in the entertainment industry.
Also my friend Roy Booth.
Without him, it would never have happened.

— PROLOGUE —

What the hell am I doing here? I thought, as I stood nervously in the club dressing room, waiting to go on stage for the first time in so many years.

My life had been full of ups and downs from the day I sang my first song at the *2i's* Coffee Bar in London in 1958.

I had worked with top producers, had a recording career, played on scores of records, brushed shoulders with the stars, even worked with many of them. I had lived in the best part of London in the best decade to live. Now here I was in the twilight of my career, all alone, waiting to go on stage and make my comeback.

Why had I let myself be talked in this? I thought. *I can't hack it. That's it, I'm off.*

Just as I was about to leave, there was a knock on the door and the compère, dressed in an old fashioned velvet suit, entered the room.

'Everything all right, Rog?'

'Yeah,' I replied.

'Didn't you used to be wi...'

'Probably,' I replied, cutting the compère short.

'Who knows where this will lead to?'

I nodded graciously, but didn't smile. I'd had my time.

'Anyway, half an hour till you kill 'em!'

— CHAPTER ONE —

Home in the Valleys

They used to call rock and roll the Devil's music, but I was born on All Saints Day, November 1st, just missing Halloween. There were just three people present at my birth in that grey stoned terraced house in the mining village of Llanbradach, Rhymney Valley, South Wales. Present were my mother, Doreen; my grandmother Martha; and the midwife. My father, Jim, was in the British Army, fighting for his country somewhere in Europe.

The house was a typical three bedroom, stone-built terraced house in the south Wales valleys. It had three rooms downstairs including the kitchen: all three downstairs rooms had flagstone floors, the three wooden bedroom floors were covered in lino, and all rooms had small coal fire-grates installed.

At the back of the house was a beautiful long garden, filled on one side with red and white rose bushes, on the other with blackcurrant and redcurrant bushes, and at the bottom with an outside toilet. If you worked in the coalmines you were allowed so many tons of coal a year. Our coalhouse had a square wooden door the size of a small window. This could be opened to allow you to shovel coal through from the back lane.

The kitchen fireplace had a heated side oven and a hob

on which a kettle was permanently placed. In the corner of the kitchen was the pantry: a room under the stairs where all the food was kept. This held all the food my parent's ration book would allow them to buy. Milk was delivered by horse and cart, and fresh hot bread came from the local bakery. I used to love the hot bread with margarine. We only ate butter on special occasions.

I will never forget the metallic brown box my father always carried with him when he returned home on leave, and the smell of the dark chocolate that wafted up from inside it. Then there were the clogs from Holland with my name painted on them (I still have them), the wooden American jeep with a star on the bonnet, and the Mont Blanc fountain pen that he had acquired for my mother.

In my later years I mystified my parents with these memories. I can't have been much more than a baby. But I've always had a good memory; it's served me well writing this book! I can remember starting school at Coed-Y-Brain Infant's School and my teacher having a sort of extra thumb growing from the joint of one of her normal thumbs. I was fascinated by it; every time she spoke to me, I found myself staring at it. I remember her telling me off many times for this. I was a shy young child and never really mixed with the other children. When I was around four or five, I was sitting with my mother on a bench next to a sand pit. Nearby other children were happily playing with their buckets and spades, but not me. My mother turned to me and said, 'I'll put my hands over my eyes and count to ten, and when I open them, I want to see you in the sand pit with your bucket and spade.' I watched her put her hand over her eyes and slowly count to ten: 'One, two, three…' She opened her eyes and *surprise*: I was still on the bench next to her.

At the age of six, and with my father safely back home, we moved to the cattle-market village of Nelson, around four to five miles north of Llanbradach. My parents were given the tenancy of a two-bedroom council prefab which had a small fridge installed in the kitchen. It was the first time we had ever seen one. My father had to separate the larger bedroom into two: one for me, and another, just large enough to accommodate a single bed and a cabinet, for my sister, Cheryl. Food was still on ration, as were sweets and chocolate. I can vividly remember my mother tearing a two-point ration coupon from our family ration book and giving me a few pennies to buy some sweets. And I will never forget the day that sweets came off ration. It was 1953. I had been saving some money my grandmother and uncle had given me. As I entered the sweet shop, with two half crowns in my pocket, my eyes lit up. I could buy whatever sweets and chocolate I wanted! I felt very lucky.

I passed my eleven-plus and attended Caerphilly Grammar Technical School, where I learned absolutely nothing (my own fault). Oh! Except Welsh, which I have now mostly forgotten. Rather than going to school I would inevitably end up in one of the local billiard halls.

One incident from my schooldays stands out in particular – and perhaps sums up the entirety of my time there. One day in 1958, our school was playing a rival school at rugby, and a friend and I had decided to turn up and show our support. But soon we became bored and noticed that beside us, on our vantage of a bank of grass, was a heavy roller used to flatten the pitch. I told my friend to push it down the bank. He didn't have enough strength so I helped him. We watched as it thundered towards the scrum. We knew we'd gone too far and began shouting loudly and waving our arms to attract the attention of the players. Luckily, a few of the players realised what was happening and alerted the others in time. The scrum scattered in every direction. Summoned to Mr Bell Jones's, the headmaster's, office, we were told in no uncertain terms that today, we – shall we say – could leave the school slightly earlier than originally planned.

And soon I was gone for good. By the summer, at the age of fifteen, I was out of school and delivering groceries on a bicycle, working part time for Thomas and Evans and Pegler's grocery stores. In the evenings, in Nelson, there were two main meeting places: the local youth club, which had opened in Llanfabon Primary School, and Frank's café, located at the corner of High Street and Shingrig Road. Frank was a stocky bald Italian, who as you approached the counter, would appear as if by magic from a side room. In those days, there would be an Italian café in nearly every village and town in the south Wales valleys. The Italian workers had come over in their droves when the Welsh mines were booming. One thing Frank had done was to install a jukebox. It was three pence a play or five plays for a shilling. I used to stand in the doorway of the café listening to all the new pop records, staring out into the night, utterly enraptured by what I heard. I could not play an instrument, and the only time I had sung was in school, but I knew – from the first time I heard Elvis Presley's voice. I wanted to be like one of the singers on the jukebox.

One day my friend, Ken Hope invited me to join him

on a football trip to London – Cardiff were playing Fulham. He quickly changed his mind though and announced, 'Stuff the football match. We'll hit the West End.' I jumped at the chance.

— CHAPTER TWO —

My First Taste of London

After an early start we arrived at Paddington Station just after midday. Ken and his mates worked for the railway at the Caerphilly railway sheds, so a group of us headed down on the cheap.

Off Ken's mates went to the football match, whilst Ken, myself, and two other guys hit the town. Our first port of call was the West End and a good pub. Many years later, after living in London, I realised it must have been *The George* in Wardour Street. I remember hiding at the back of the bar behind a crowd of people; it was November, and I had just turned sixteen, but I looked a lot younger. Ken was the same age as me, but he was taller, bigger, and not so baby-faced – so he was on bar duty. I started knocking back the lager and lime, and after about an hour we decided to find somewhere to eat. I wanted to find the *2i's* Coffee Bar – the place where British rock 'n' roll had started – but the others just wanted to move from pub to pub getting the drink down them.

We were strolling through an alleyway, which I now recognise as St Anne's Court, looking for a place to eat, when suddenly a woman appeared out of a doorway and asked Ken if he would like a good time. Ken replied, 'I'm having a great time already!'

She continued, 'No, a *really* good time. It'll cost you ten shillings.' She held her hand out.

'Ten bob!' cried Ken, 'No, I don't think so,' but the other two guys were egging him on. 'Go on, Ken, dip your wick,' they said.

'Why don't *you*?!' shouted Ken at his friends.

'She asked you first!'

'I don't trust her boys. She wants the money up front.'

But then Ken had a great idea (or so he thought). He tore a ten-shilling note in half, handed her one half and said, 'Here's five bob. You can have the other half after we do it.' Whereupon, a man stepped out of the darkness. He was of average size, had black slicked-back hair, and was wearing a heavy camel-type coat. In his hand he had a flick knife.

He stood in front of Ken, who was himself around two yards in front of us, and blurted, 'You trying to be fucking funny? You taking the piss?'

One of the two guys with us, Jim, was around thirty years of age, a big guy, an ex-miner; he put himself between the two men and took the half note off Ken. 'He's right, let her have the other half of the note. You can't do things like that.' He offered it to the woman – 'Here you are, love.' – but just as he was about to hand it over, he head-butted the guy with the knife, who staggered back and then went down. Then grabbing the half note from the woman he turned back to us and said, 'Right, let's get something to eat!'

We legged it as fast as we could. I found out later they called him Big Jim, and was told that when he ate eggs he would also eat the shells. When I asked him why he ate the eggshells, he said that when he swallowed the crunched-up shells, they would cut the heads off the germs in his throat, and that was the reason why he never ever had bad throats. *Something wrong here*, I thought.

We eventually found a café in Charing Cross Road, not far from Denmark Street. Denmark Street was nicknamed *Tin Pan Alley*. It was a street full of music publishers, a small club, and two recording studios. I would be spending a considerable amount of time here in the future. After, with full stomachs, and having found the pub opposite closed, I finally got my way and we headed for the *2i's*.

Tommy Steele had started singing in the *2i's* in 1956. *Cliff Richard and the Drifters* (later called *Cliff Richard and the Shadows*) had been there in the summer, just a few months earlier. Then there was Adam Faith, *Johnny Kidd (and The Pirates)*, Ritchie Blackmore, Paul Gadd (Gary Glitter) – the list of those who frequented the club was like a who's who of the soon to be huge. Not to mention the movers and shakers, the people destined to leave their mark behind the scenes: Lionel Bart, who was writing rock songs at the time, and music promoters such as Larry Parnes, Jack Good and Don Arden (Sharon Osbourne's father). The *2i's* had been named after Freddie and Sammy Irani, who had been the previous owners, but in 1956 it had been taken over by Ray Hunter and Paul Lincoln, an Australian wrestler known as Dr Death. In 1958, Tom Littlewood, previously the doorman at the *2i's*, became its manager. I did not know at the time, but fast-forwarding six years, Tom Littlewood would become a big influence on my life.

On our arrival I was surprised to find how small the coffee bar really was. It was just a little bigger than Frank's café back home. On the walls there were photographs and posters of the pop stars who had performed there, but I was a little disappointed that we were not allowed downstairs to see the room where the groups played. It was closed until the evening. At least Ken didn't seem too fazed. 'Let's get pissed!' he declared.

Two pubs later we found Big Jim and Alan, with three girls, knocking back the booze like there was no tomorrow. As we joined them, Ken started speaking to me in Welsh. He wasn't a Welsh speaker – he only knew the lord's Prayer – and I had only been taught enough Welsh at school for the most basic of exchanges. But between us we could hold something that to non-Welsh speakers appeared a normal conversation. We did this, of course, to impress the girls.

'Oh, you speak a foreign language?' asked one of the girls.

'Yeah,' Ken replied.

'What language is that?' she said.

Jim butted in. 'God's own language, love: Welsh.'

'We hate the Welsh!' came a man's voice a few tables away.

'Who the fuck said that?' Jim yelled, scanning around the bar.

'I did,' came the reply. I looked across to see around six or seven blokes, Londoners I assumed. Anyway, the one shouting off had a cockney accent.

'And I hate the fucking English!' shouted Jim. I looked at Ken and he looked at me. We were both thinking the same thing: *Uh oh, we're fucked!*

Jim shouted something back, I cannot remember exactly what. Then the locals started getting to their feet. This is it, I thought. Jim was a big fellow and, as we had witnessed earlier, could obviously handle himself. I could not tell with

Alan: he was tall but a bit thinner than Jim. Ken was tall and gangly but would have a go at anybody. And while, with the lager in me, I felt about six foot four and fourteen stone, I wasn't yet pissed enough to forget that really I was shorter than Ken and nine stone nothing. The locals were heading towards us, and they did not look happy. We didn't know if they had flick knives (which were commonly carried in those days), knuckle dusters in their pockets, bike chains under their jackets… We rose nervously to our feet but just as I thought it was all about to kick off, a voice with a broad Scottish accent bellowed out, 'We hate the English too!'

The locals stopped dead in their tracks and looked in the direction of the voice, as did we. There, crowding the bar, was a gang of Scottish guys and three Scottish girls. They did not look the type you wanted to argue with. The pub went silent.

It seemed an age before Alan said, 'C'mon let's forget it. We all say things when we've had a drink, all right boys?'

From the looks on their faces, I wasn't sure the Scottish guys were going to be satisfied with that. But then one of the Scottish girls turned to the guy who had shouted and said. 'C'mon, get the drinks in. I'm dying of thirst here.' Turning to the local boys and us, she said, 'Let's all have a drink. We didn't mean all that crap.'

The locals sat back down and I think we all breathed a sigh of relief. We drank up, made our excuses and left, saying goodbye to the Scottish boys on the way out. One of them turned and said, 'You're not stopping for a wee one then?'

I replied, 'No we've got a train to catch.' God knows what happened there after we left.

*

We made our way back to the *2i's* and by then it was packed. Ken and I managed to squeeze in but Jim and Alan were left behind in the press. They were shouting after us, asking us to come back out; it wasn't their scene anyway, they didn't want to hang around, especially as there were so many pubs nearby to choose from. Ken shouted back, telling them to go ahead, we'd catch up.

We barged our way downstairs, though not before being charged a shilling entrance fee.

I couldn't believe it. *I'm actually here.* This was the room where Tommy Steele, Adam Faith, and *Cliff Richard and The Shadows* had been discovered. I hadn't expected it to be so small! I just stood there drinking in the atmosphere. You could smell the sweat. I can only describe it as like rush hour on the tube: everyone so close to each other you could practically feel the heat. As the band played the punters tried to dance, but it was so full that none of us could really move. It was a sea of bodies bobbing up and down; there was no way they could move sideways; there was more room in a tin of sardines. I noticed there was a delivery hatch in the ceiling above and asked a guy next to me why they didn't open it. 'Too cold this time of year. They only open it in the summer,' came the reply.

I took it all in, lost in my amazement. I don't know how long I was stood there before Ken's shouting cut through my reverie. 'C'mon, let's go. We've seen it now. The band's crap.'

'No, not yet. I want to say I sang here.'

'It's just a caf,' said Ken.

But I couldn't come all this way and not sing.

As the band finished their number Ken, realising there

was no other way to get me to the next pub, shouted out to them, 'Oi, butty, this little twat wants to sing,'

'What does he know?' came the reply. I told Ken to tell them 'All Shook Up' or 'Singing The Blues'. They were fed up with that 'Singing the Blues' – everyone wanted to do it. So they let me get up and sing the Elvis number. I was in a daze. I had dreamed of this moment so many times. I can't remember what I was thinking. Probably I wasn't thinking much of anything at all. But when the band came in I knew what to do. I opened my mouth and started to sing. As far as I know, it was in the same key as Elvis sang it, and from the reaction of the audience, it seemed to go well.

After the applause subsided, the lead guitarist wanted to know where I was from.

'Wales,' I replied.

'Then piss off back! You're too good for this place,' he responded with a grin.

Brilliant! I'd just sang at the birthplace of British Rock 'n' Roll. We struggled back upstairs and out into the fresh air. Joining back up with Jim and Alan, we headed for Kings Cross to book in at a B&B, found a pub and stayed there until closing time then headed for bed.

Sat on the train home the next day, watching the Berkshire countryside roll by, I thought over the past twenty-four hours. It had certainly been an eventful trip. I felt like I'd learned a few things: for one thing, don't mess with a pimp. Or the Scots, for that matter. And although there was one thing I supposed I had already known, I was now more sure of it than I'd ever been: I wanted to be a pop star!

— CHAPTER THREE —

The Day I Very Nearly Joined the Army

On my return home, my father found me a job at the local garage as a trainee mechanic. I earned two pounds a week. On payday, Friday, I gave my mother a pound and would keep a pound for myself.

On the Tuesday she would give me ten shillings back, so that I could go to the *EMP* (*Empress Ballroom*) in Abercynon, where every Tuesday and Saturday they would hold a dance. There were many of these dance halls situated around the valleys in south Wales, held in a variety of old and sometimes new buildings. Wherever they could hold a dance they would. At the *EMP* they played records through a small Dansette record player; sometimes they would book an occasional group to play on the Saturday evening. The groups would become more popular as time went on, but for now, it would be mostly dancing to the old record player.

Ten shillings in those days could buy quite a lot of drink. A pint of beer cost around one and a penny. For those who weren't around at the time that would be one old shilling and an old penny. When you think that there were twenty shillings to the pound, and twelve pence to the shilling, ten shillings would buy nine pints of beer and you would still have three pence left. It would cost a shilling or two to get into the dance, buy some cigarettes, and then keep a little back for some chips on the way home, you could still down six or seven pints, more if you bought rough cider, which was only around seven to nine pence a pint.

I would have been classed as a Ted, (Teddy Boy). Teds traditionally wore drainpipe trousers (trousers or jeans that tapered to a tight fit at the ankles), long jackets that usually had a velvet collar – the length of the jacket would always be measured down to the bottom of the little finger with the arm positioned straight down at the side – black suede thick crepe-souled shoes, fluorescent green, yellow or pink socks (some Ted's didn't wear those) a string tie, and the compulsory DA (Ducks Arse), also called the Tony Curtis haircut, named after the film star. This would be greased back and combed each side at the back of the head into what looked like a ducks arse, then, you would get your fingers and pull your hair forward at the front. Teds were so-called, because the look was similar in appearance to the male attire of the Edwardian era. The two main suit colours were either blue with a black velvet collar and sometimes velvet cuffs or, black with a matching black velvet collar. Mine was mostly black, although I did have one blue suit made. My parents never really liked me wearing these clothes but, I was part of the gang and that was it.

The music played at the *EMP* would be current chart hits by Elvis, Cliff Richard, Buddy Holly, Little Richard, Jerry Lee Lewis, Marty Wilde etc and the jive was the dance. I remember vividly, leaning against the wall inside the dance hall, cigarette in the side of my mouth jiving with one of the girls. I say jiving; she was doing all the movements, swinging herself around one way then the other, twisting herself around as my arm stretched over her head, whilst I just smoked the cigarette with my left hand as I leant against the wall. As the music finished and she waltzed back to her gang of girls, I heard her declare, 'Go and have a jive with him, he's bloody marvellous.'

I remember a few of the groups who started playing at the *EMP*. There were *The Astronauts* a tight three-piece outfit who sang and played instrumentals, I believe they were from the Aberdare area. Then around 1962 *Tommy Scott and the Senators* emerged from Pontypridd. Tommy later changed his name to Tom Jones. *The Strollers*, another Pontypridd outfit, and I believe *The Bystanders* from Merthyr Tydfil played the *EMP*, although I never got to see them play. Watching these groups made me even more determined to make it in the music business.

The job at the garage did not last long. I was doing fine until the mechanic (they only employed one) said to me, 'When you go for lunch today, take the motorbike instead of walking.' The bike was a sleek, gleaming silver number, with a long leather sebat and an exhaust pipe that tapered at the end like the mouthpiece of a saxophone. Though it was propped in the corner of the garage, it wasn't something we were working on; it belonged to my boss. I jumped at the mechanic's offer. I had learned to ride on a friend's motorbike six months previously and had been longing to try this one out.

I was about halfway home when I saw a big car coming towards me on the opposite side of the road. It was being driven by the garage owner. I waved to him, and he waved back at me. But when I got back to the garage, I found out that he had not realised that it was me riding the bike, and he sacked me for taking it without his permission, and for riding without a driving license and insurance. So that was it for my career as a mechanic. I suppose it was for the best. If I'd been cut out for it, I imagine I would be able to remember the brand of the motorcycle which got me fired!

At the time, an older friend had been called up for national service, which meant serving in the forces for two years. The system ended in 1960, meaning that all children born after October 1939 were spared. My friends and I thanked our lucky stars. But it didn't stop Ken and I, one Friday evening, trying to sign up of our own accord. We had spent most of the afternoon drinking in *The Bridge* pub, which is now Pontypridd police station. But, strolling down the road towards the railway station we caught sight of the recruitment office and before I knew it we were inside and Ken was signing up with his real name, Kenneth Hope, his real address, and telling the bemused recruitment officer that he wanted a gun as soon as possible. I signed up as Charles Drake (Charlie Drake was a well-known comedian at the time) gave a false address, and the recruitment officer never batted an eyelid. We had forgotten all about it until the military arrived at Ken's home.

There was nothing I could do but stand and watch as they led him away. He caught my eye and started shouting 'What about him? Roger Simmonds!'

'Never heard of him,' came the reply. Eventually, Ken's parents did manage to find a way to get him discharged from the army. I believe in those days, because he had not long joined, you were allowed to pay a certain amount of money. Anyway, the outcome was that Ken was forbidden from associating with me anymore. But that didn't last long.

*

It was easy to get jobs in those days. You could leave one job and start another the following week. At the time, Ken and I would try to get work with the same company, which we managed on numerous occasions. The jobs went on and on, one after the other. A soft drinks factory, then a nylon spinner's factory, a building site in Pontypridd, a building site at *Llanwern Steel Works* in Newport, a sheet metal works factory, a factory making oil tanks... the list was endless.

I just wanted to get away again, be a part of the music scene. Not just any scene, *the* scene: the only scene, the London scene. And it wasn't exactly in commuting distance. Ken said he would move with me, but in the end decided against it. So I decided to wait until I'd saved enough to make sure I could survive for a while. I could sell some of my possessions to add to the fund, and as soon as I had enough money I would be off. If the worst came to the worst, I thought, I could always stay with my Aunty Glad and Uncle Harold; they lived in Hayes, Middlesex, the place where my mother and father had first met, and where I had spent a lovely holiday with them back in my childhood. By the second week of October 1959, I thought I had saved enough, and I booked my ticket, one way, to London.

The day I was planning to leave, my sister, Cheryl, somehow got wind of it. None of us can quite remember how she found out. Ken might have told his brother Terry and he might have told Cheryl. Cheryl was eleven at the time and I can remember her running down the road after me, yelling and pleading with me to come back home. But I was adamant. I was going. Sat in the bus I looked back at her, standing there at the bus stop. She was seemingly still shouting, but with the noise of the engine and the passengers talking, I couldn't hear a thing. I was on my way to Cardiff, then London, and no one was going to stop me!

— CHAPTER FOUR —

The 2i's Coffee Bar

It was late afternoon when I arrived at the *2i's*. I ordered a coffee and thought to myself, *what do I do now?* Had it been the right decision to come to London on my own? I had spent the early afternoon touring the local coffee bars and pubs, but after only these few short hours, I was already beginning to feel I'd made a mistake. I was sixteen, but a young sixteen, and I looked about fourteen. I probably wouldn't even get served at half these places, let alone allowed on stage.

However, for the time being I needed a place to stay. I had decided to try the B&B in Kings Cross where I had stayed with Ken and the boys on my previous visit. Having booked in, I started back, on foot, towards Gower Street. It was dark, chilly, and drizzling with rain, and I believe it was on Gower street that I decided to catch a bus that would drop me at New Oxford Street. It was just a short walk from there to the *2i's,* but as I hurriedly walked through the rain-soaked streets, I began to lose my bearings.

What the hell am I doing here? I thought, as I sheltered in a shop doorway. It was not cold, just chilly, but the rain had soaked me to my skin, and I was shivering. And it didn't help that I had not eaten. I was cold, hungry and miserable. I eventually asked at a newspaper kiosk and they gave me directions to Old Compton Street. On the way, I found a fish and chip shop and ordered a fish and double portion of chips. The rain by now had eased a little, and I cut through to Dean Street eating my chips. The wet streets lined with old cars reminded me of black and white British gangster films. I stopped and admired a Mark VIII Jaguar glistening wet, parked under a street lamp outside a club. As I gazed through the window two fellows dressed identically in long black raincoats tied with belts at the waist emerged from the club, told me in no uncertain terms to piss off, got in to the car, and drove away. I had always loved cars and vowed there and then that one day I would own a Mark VIII Jaguar. Then, before I knew it, I was on familiar ground, the lights of the *2i's* sign twinkling ahead of me. Full of chips and starting to dry, I began to feel a bit better about things.

I returned every night to the *2i's* and began to make friends with the regulars. My days were spent walking around Oxford Street and Regent Street, visiting the big stores – at least they were warm inside. I would then frequent one of the pubs, where a pint of beer would last me for a few hours. After that I would usually grab fish and chips and head back to the *2i's*.

It was starting to become a little dull. I desperately needed to have a band of my own. Then by chance, one evening in the *2i's*, I met Mike Pratt. The band of a friend of Mike's was playing that night and he had popped in to see what they were like. I was awestruck when he told me that he was a friend of Lionel Bart and had been involved in writing the first British rock ' n' roll song in 1956, *Rock With The Caveman* by Tommy Steele. I had listened to *Rock With The Caveman* more times than I could count. Although

I never owned a copy of the record, a friend of mine had bought it, and both he and I had played it so many times that it had nearly worn away. We had a single-play record player, and as the inside electrics and the plastic casing got hot with the constant plays, it would emit an odour so acrid that I can still remember it to this day. At the time I had had no idea who the songwriter was. We were only interested in the person singing.

But I knew better by then, of course. I stood in awe listening to Mike telling me what he had lined up for the future. He even offered me advice. He told me to either join a group as a singer, or even better, to learn to play an instrument, such as guitar or keyboard. By learning to play an instrument, I could write my own songs and become totally independent. Here was the guy whose song I knew note for note advising little old me on how to become a pop star. This was the kind of thing I'd been hoping for in moving to London. It was fascinating talking to him. I would never see Mike again, but years later he would become well known for playing the part of Jeff in the series *Randall and Hopkirk (Deceased)*, which also starred Kenneth Cope.

London was a sea of coffee bars, clip joints and strip clubs. Just two years previously, the business venture of a certain Paul Raymond, *Raymond's Review Bar*, had opened in Walkers Court. In later years Raymond would become known as Britain's richest man, a one man tabloid scandal whose empire of dirty magazines and dirty bars scandalised (and titillated) the nation for forty years. But back then he was just one of the thousands of young men looking to make their fortune in London, and *Raymond's Revue Bar* had to compete with the likes of the iconic *Windmill Theatre*. But it was already causing a stir. At the *Windmill Theatre*, the girls would just sit or stand naked without any movement whatsoever – this had been the law for years. However, because *Raymond's Revue Bar* was a private members' club, the naked girls could move. It's fair to say that this was considered an improvement: a spate of strip joints opened following this model. Though *The Windmill* was not famous only for its nude shows; it had been the birthplace of such comedy geniuses as Tony Hancock, Peter Sellers, Bruce Forsyth and Tommy Cooper, amongst many others. Alas, it closed in the latter half of 1964, though it did reopen as a cinema a little while later. I did get to see a show there just before it closed, though my memory of it is a little hazy, as we were all drunk at the time.

After nearly a week in London I was getting a little bored of being on my own. I had worked out that if I didn't earn any money I could probably survive another seven or eight nights at a push. Tom Littlewood, the manager of the *2i's*, told me to get myself a group, 'The days of the solo singer are numbered.' Tom had slicked back, greased, black hair and always wore a brown faded suit. It had a unusual sheen, as if it had been ironed one too many times, and was dotted here and there by a few stains that seemed to blend into the fabric. Tom also informed me that he was a Judo expert. Between this and the fact that the two owners were wrestlers, it was not surprising that there was hardly ever any trouble in the coffee bar.

One evening, I got talking to a guy named Martin. He was a guitarist from the Nottingham area and told me he had worked for Larry Parnes, backing a few of his singers.

He asked what I did.

'Nothing at the moment,' I said. 'I want to get into the music business. I think I can sing. I know a few songs, but that's it.'

He told me that later on he would be jamming with a few musicians, and if I wanted I could get up and give a song. 'What songs do you know?' he asked. I reeled off a few. 'Can't do that one, that's one of Cliff's... Can't do that one, that's one of Marty's...'

Eventually I said, 'If I'm getting up I'm either doing *Move It* or *Great Balls of Fire*. Later that evening I watched as Martin and a few other musicians started jamming. He was a good guitarist, much better than I thought he would be, and together they were really rocking. After about twenty minutes, he called a girl up to sing. She sang a song I had never heard before, the crowd didn't like it, and she walked off to silence. They played a few more numbers, and then it was my turn.

' "Great Balls of Fire",' he said. 'What key do you do it in?'

'Don't know,' I said. 'Play "Move It" in Cliff Richard's key.' But they started *Great Balls of Fire*. I tried to come in but couldn't get in key. I had never sang the song on stage before. They kept playing the intro waiting for me to come in. I tried again – it was near enough for jazz, as they say. I went down worse than the girl. I could not believe that just the previous year, when I had sang *All Shook Up*, I brought the place down. I was about to take my exit when Martin started playing *Move It*. I was still nervous but got through it in key. I got a great response from the crowd, which really lifted me. Martin turned to me and said, 'You have something there – work on it.'

Back in those days my parents didn't have a telephone. In fact, no one we knew did, so I had written to them to tell them that I had arrived safely. Sometimes, on the off chance, I would ring the phone box outside the *Hollybush* pub in Nelson, and if someone answered, I would ask them to nip down to my parents' house, which was not too far away, and tell them I would phone back in half an hour. When I rang back either my mother or father would be waiting in the telephone box to take my call. I would always tell them how well I was doing, but deep down I believe they knew it wasn't true.

I sang again at the *2i's*, now with a little more confidence; a fantastic group backed me and this time we were in the right key. I was beginning to click with the crowd. In those days if you went down well at the *2i's*, there would be many so-called managers coming out of the woodwork trying to sign you up. The following evening, one such manager introduced himself. He was an ex-newspaper reporter named Eddie. Eddie had worked for numerous papers in the past, and after interviewing most of the top managers in the music business, he'd thought *if they can do it so can I*. Eddie said I could be the new Laurie London. Laurie London had had a huge hit in 1958 with an American spiritual song entitled *He's Got The Whole World In His Hands*. It reached number one in the British charts and number two in the American charts and had become one of the most successful records released by a British male singer in America during the 1950s. Laurie London sang ballads, and

I sang rock ' n' roll, so Eddie said we wouldn't clash.

The only problem was that Eddie thought that I was around fourteen. As I have already mentioned, I looked young for my age. In fact, the following week I would turn seventeen. But worried that he would call the whole thing off if he knew, I didn't correct him. Eddie was pushing to meet my parents so they could give their permission for him to start the ball rolling. He was also getting some contracts for me to sign. It shouldn't be a problem; after all, didn't I live in King's Cross with my family? I was trying to put him off. He told me he had contacts in the recording industry and that he could do a deal with Larry Parnes. Larry was the top manager in the business. He'd managed Tommy Steele, Marty Wilde, Georgie Fame, and Joe Brown, and it just so happened that Eddie knew Larry very well. Parnes would go on to manage *The Viscounts*, one of whom was Gordon Mills, who went on to manage Tom Jones. I made up excuse after excuse as to why my parents weren't available. For now, he said that he would proceed with things until we signed the contracts, though in the meantime I would need to learn new songs. I, on the other hand, could not keep up the pretence. Time was ticking and I was fast running out of money; I was planning to return home on my seventeenth birthday.

To save money I decided to spend a few nights on Euston Station. Many struggling musicians made for either Euston or Kings Cross station to spend the night. You would not be able to do that today with all the security around. I met a couple of musicians there who were from the North East and a good laugh. They had heard of Hank Marvin and

Bruce Welch's success with Cliff Richard and had thought they would head for London, and the *2i's*, to emulate their success. I could only stick two nights sleeping rough in the station. I wasn't equipped for it; I didn't have any real winter clothing: just a few jumpers and a leather jacket. The weather was becoming much colder; I had to get back to the hotel. I had kept enough money back for my fare home and scraped enough together to buy some food and to spend two more nights at the B&B.

The evening before I was to return home, Eddie informed me that an associate of his from the Larry Parnes office had been in to listen to me sing. Unfortunately, when this person had told Larry about me, Larry had said he wasn't interested as I was too young. He was looking for someone a bit older than fourteen. Someone around the age of seventeen or eighteen who would appeal to the girls. I couldn't believe my luck! I confessed to Eddie that I would soon be turning seventeen, and I had only gone along with him because I thought I would have a better chance of succeeding if I kept up the pretence. Now he knew I was nearly seventeen, maybe he could get me a deal with Larry Parnes. He took the news well, wished me luck, and said that it didn't matter if I *was* seventeen: he wanted somebody who *looked* seventeen and was seventeen. So that was it, it was goodbye to the *2i's* and to London. I arrived home just in time to blow out the candles on my birthday cake.

— CHAPTER FIVE —

The Z Men

My parents were glad to see me back. Within a week I was doing shift work in a factory on the Treforest Industrial Estate near Pontypridd, earning very good money and saving to buy a guitar and amplifier.

While I had been away, Ken had decided to form a band. He had been learning to play guitar and had roped in another friend (also named Ken). Ken (Hope, my mate) decided to be the lead guitarist, with the other Ken on the rhythm guitar. I didn't have much choice. I became the bass guitar player. We acquired our instruments from Frank Wride, who owned a music shop in Pontypridd. My bass was a Rossetti Lucky Seven, probably one of the best of the cheaper basses around at the time. I later found out that Paul McCartney used the solid version of the Lucky Seven. I had no idea how to play a bass and learning was a slow process. We would practise individually and then meet up twice a week at the local social club to rehearse. I would spend all of my free time shut in my bedroom running up and down scales. If I was going to play the bass guitar then I wanted to be as good as I possibly could. But after months of practise we seemed to be getting nowhere. When we met up for rehearsals, we would always make mistakes. I had heard through the grapevine that a group in the next village,

The Comancheros, were looking for a bass player. I found out where and what nights they rehearsed, and turned up one evening to see them. After taking some time to think, they got back to me, and I was in. This was probably late 1960, early 1961.

The two Kens were not pleased. They called me a traitor and didn't speak to me for a long while, but I knew I was going nowhere with them. Though what I did not know at the time was that in three years I would be working with Ken Hope once again, but this time it would be at the most famous club in the world.

I was at last being paid to be on stage and was happy working with the new group. We had a good front singer and were doing well, getting regular bookings. One Sunday evening a band mate suggested we go over to Blackwood, Gwent, for a drink. 'They've got some good entertainment at *The Royal Oak*,' he said. It was here I met a lifelong friend, and the man who was to have the greatest influence on my music career. As we approached we could hear music coming from inside. And not just any music. Standing in the smoke-filled back room, a guitar slung around his neck, was a tubby guy. He reminded me a bit of Eddie Cochran. He was playing a Hofner Club 60 electric guitar and had a guitar amplifier sat on the table next to him. His plump fingers, what I could see of them, were moving so fast they were just a blur. I had never heard anyone play guitar like this before. He used what they call an open tuning and had learned to play his own style of chord structures. I thought he was amazing. I could not believe the sound this guy was creating. I had listened to the lead guitarists at the *2i's* and they were good, but nothing compared to this bloke. Before leaving I managed to have a quick chat with him. He told me his name was Roy Booth and that he lived in Blackwood. We left, but our paths were soon to cross again.

For weeks, months, I kept thinking about that guitarist from Blackwood; the way he played, the sound he made was so different. No one in Britain was playing the music he played, not even the top rock and blues bands. Then in early '62, myself and Ken Hope (he had forgiven me by then for leaving his group) were drinking scrumpy in *The Hollybush Inn*, Nelson. We had been there for a couple of hours and were well on our way. I remember that Ken was chatting up a girl I had christened Scrumpy Lil, as I had never seen any girl drink scrumpy as she could. But before long, when Lil went to powder her nose, Ken turned to me and said, 'Let's go. She's starting to drink me under the table!' He suggested we head for the local dance. 'Pull a couple of birds,' he said.

As we neared the *Wingfield Hall*, the music floating out into the night was note perfect. 'No group on tonight,' Ken said, 'it's a record playing.' But when we entered the hall, on stage was Roy, the guy I had seen in Blackwood. This time he had a full band behind him: a rhythm guitarist, a bass player, and a drummer. The drummer was standing, hammering the hell out of his drum kit, and had his bass drum lit up. He was the heaviest drummer I had ever heard. In fact, it was the loudest group I had ever heard. My first thoughts were, *I have to join this lot!*

I did not have to wait long. At the end of the evening I got talking to Jeff, the rhythm guitarist. He told me the bass player was giving up the music business. I explained to him that I was a bass player and I wanted to join his outfit. He asked what group I was in, but when I told him he replied, 'Never heard of them.'

He went to speak to Roy, who said, 'So you're a bass player. Are you any good?'

'Yeah,' I replied. 'I think so.'

'No good thinking you're good. You have to be *good* to join this band.'

So I ended up in Blackwood one afternoon at one of their rehearsals, and I was in. We played the local clubs and our 'following' soon began to grow. We were playing a heavier type of music than the run-of-the-mill groups that were on the scene, with our own arrangements of the typical songbook of the day. A short, dark Italian-looking singer called Lenny fronted the group. Lenny could sing any type of song from rock, blues, and ballads to the standards. We were called *Lenny and The Z Men* and we were on a roll.

The loss of Lenny came after a competition at one of the clubs. We would participate in these whenever we needed to earn some extra money. We would always enter as a group but Lenny would also enter as a solo singer. This was very much against the rules, but we would try to appear towards the beginning of the competition and Lenny towards the end. There was only one problem with this: the clubs in those days usually employed a pianist or organist to back the solo singers, and some of them were not very good, to say the least. Lenny would always want us backing him. How the judges never noticed baffled me.

The group had been getting better and better. We were now a tight and professional outfit, and although I say it myself, I had not heard a better group in the south Wales area. We came first. The three judges said that we were the best group they had ever heard. But they criticised Lenny's solo appearance, saying he was throwing his arms about so much they thought he was having a seizure. Soon afterwards Lenny finished with us. He was a great showman and singer and we all missed him. He ended up living near Blackpool, where he opened a flower shop. He continued singing, and had a good following on the Blackpool club circuit. I went to see him perform at one of Blackpool clubs a while back and he was still great.

So now it was just *The Z Men*. Me on bass, Jinx the drummer, Jeff Williams rhythm guitar, and Roy Booth on lead guitar. We were getting fed up playing locally, but all the same, we were doing well. We had a residency, once a month at *The New Moon Club* in Cardiff, which was situated at the bottom of the Hayes. The owner, Ted, had briefly managed Shirley Bassey in the days when she sang in the local workingmen's clubs. We got on well with Ted and his son Peter and they started to give us more work.

We were playing at *The New Moon Club* the day President Kennedy was assassinated (November 22nd 1963). Two weeks later, we were at *The New Moon Club* on a social night out. A rival band from Blackwood, *The Vampires*, were playing and we wanted to see them perform. *The Vampires* had a huge following and, unbeknownst to us, had secured some local television work – they were going places! Unfortunately their bass player failed to turn up, so one of them came over to ask me if I would fill in for him. 'Let 'em struggle!' said Jeff, but in the end we all agreed that I would have a go. The bass guitar and amp were already set up. I did my best, not knowing many of their numbers, and a few days later, Robert and Jerry from *The Vampires* came over to my house and offered me the gig full time (still no telephones!). I was torn; I loved the music. I was playing with *The Z Men* but *The Vampires* were making it big. They had television work coming up, and there was even talk of a weekly series, but I did not want to let our band down. I didn't know what to do.

As luck would have it, my cousin Richie had decided to pay us a visit on the day *The Vampires* called. He saw right away that I was torn, and suggested we go for a walk. *The Vampires'* van was a bit of a landmark in Blackwood back then, so he led me past it. In those days the name of a group would be painted on the side of the van, and if they had any record releases the covers would sometimes be on there as well.

On *The Vampires'* van was their name, with the words TV Stars written underneath it. Richie didn't say a word, just looked at me and pointed to those words: *TV Stars*.

I decided to join *The Vampires*. Of course, that did not go down very well with *The Z Men*, but they did manage to find a temporary replacement for me.

My time with *The Vampires* was short but sweet. In the time I was with them, we did support the bigger named bands, one of which was *Johnny Kidd and The Pirates*, who had previously had a hit with 'Shakin' All Over', a rock classic. We did television shows for the old *TWW* (*Television Wales and the West*). The main show was the afternoon program called *Gorwelion*, in which we sang in Welsh. My father, who always said I should get a proper job, was now warming to the music business. He could see I was serious about music and, with the money I was now earning, deep down he knew I would probably never go back to a day job.

I had some great laughs with *The Vampires*, and they were all excellent musicians. But one time when we were playing *The New Moon Club* my old band *The Z Men* turned up to watch us, in the interval I went over to say hello to Roy, and the first thing he said to me was, 'You're not happy with them, are you?' I don't know how he knew, but he was right! *The Vampires* were a great group and a great bunch of lads, but I was missing the sound of the Roy and the band. A week later, I was back with *The Z Men*. Ken Hope had joined us as harmonica player and vocalist, and with Roy Booth as lead guitar and lead vocalist, Jeff Williams as rhythm guitarist and backing singer, Dave Doyle on drums and backing vocalist, and me as bass player and backing singer, we now had a settled line-up. Dave Doyle had replaced Jinx as the drummer in the band as Jinx was married and had a child to look after, so had decided to give up the travelling and take a job at a local club.

We were now starting to up our game. We performed on the same bill as Charles and Kingsley Ward who later opened Rockfield recording studios (Dave Edmunds would record his number one hit, 'I hear You Knockin', there, and later it was where Queen would record 'Bohemian Rhapsody') and blew them off the stage. And as we improved as a band, the work escalated too. Soon we had to take on a road manager: Trevor. But he didn't last long; I remember giving him a pint of scrumpy. I think he had drank about three-quarters when he stood and excused himself from the table. We found him outside, crawling and mumbling along the road. We never asked him if he drank; we just assumed he did. We then took on a manger, Dave

Coombs, whose father was the local vicar. Dave was excited about managing us and went all out to get as much work as we could handle.

— CHAPTER SIX —

Liverpool Here We Come

In June 1964, we set off to play a one-nighter at a holiday camp in Pwlleli, North Wales. It was a long way to go for only one night, but we wanted to start working further afield, the money was good, and we were given overnight accommodation. We had also decided, as we were so close, to go and try our luck in Liverpool. *The Cavern Club* had taken over from the *2i's* as the number one place for groups; it had been the birthplace of *The Beatles*, and everyone wanted a shot at success. Roy and Dave were a little hesitant though, concerned about the reception we would receive. The audience were used to their own home-grown bands and their melodic style of pop songs. We, on the other hand, blasted our numbers out with a vengeance. But we had to give it a go. What did we have to lose?

The next morning, we set off early, arriving in Liverpool long before *The Cavern* was open for the lunchtime session. We sat outside for ages, and when it did open, were greeted abruptly by a miserable-looking guy who wanted to know what we were doing hanging around outside the entrance.

'We want to play here,' said Ken.

The guy raised an eyebrow. 'Who are you?'

'We're *The Z Men,* from Wales,' declared Jeff.

'Don't think any Welsh band has ever played here,' said

the guy.

'Then we'll be the first,' replied Ken.

The guy told us we would have to come back in the evening to see Bob Wooler. He said he would let Bob know we were coming and it would be up to him. We wrote our name on a piece of paper and gave it to him so he wouldn't forget, and spent the rest of the day looking around Liverpool trying to find *The Blue Angel* and many of the other well-known clubs. However, time was ticking and we had to find somewhere to stay. We ended up booking ourselves into a hostel. It was dirty and damp, but cheap.

Early evening we ventured back to *The Cavern Club*, and surprisingly we had no hassle getting in. After waiting for what seemed an eternity, we were introduced to Bob Wooler. A few years earlier, Wooler had been offered the management of *The Beatles* by Allan Williams, a former businessman, promoter and – according to his version of events anyway – *The Beatles*' first manager. Williams had himself met *The Beatles* after opening a coffee bar-cum-club called *The Jacaranda*, and he would eventually drive them to Germany for their first booking in Hamburg. During this time Williams offered Bob Wooler a job at one of his Liverpool clubs, *Top Ten Club,* but shortly after opening, it burned down. So it was while Williams was trying to build up his money supplies that he suggested Bob should manage *The Beatles*. Bob declined the offer, but eventually became instrumental in introducing *The Beatles* to Brian Epstein.

I remember thinking at the time that Bob's hair looked like a short version of a *Beatles* haircut. He was a very polite person and took an instant liking to us, and likewise, we took an instant liking to him. He said he would fix us up with a gig at a pub called *The Bear's Paw*, and if he had good reports from there, he would put us on at *The Cavern*. He pulled one of the local bands out of the *Paw* so that we could perform there the next evening. There was a great atmosphere that evening at *The Cavern*. I didn't ask the name of the group who were playing, but later one of the boy's told me it was *Earl Preston and the TT's*.

Later that evening we did the rounds, trying to cram in as much as possible of the local pubs and clubs. It was great getting to see the clubs we had heard so much about and watch the local groups, although they all seemed to be playing the same type of music. Our first day and night in Liverpool had gone well. It was a city I would revisit many times in the coming years, for work as well as pleasure.

After enjoying our evening, we made our way back to the hostel. It was a terrible place, and I wasn't feeling too good. I had a sore throat and felt as if I were coming down with the flu. The next day I felt even worse. My throat was on fire and I had a slight fever, but I was determined to do the gig and not let the others down. When we arrived at the pub that evening, it seemed dead. We were told by the bar staff it would liven up later. Sadly they lied! There were a few in, not that many, and a good deal of them were from the band we had replaced, who came along to see what we were like. We had a chat with them before we went on. To be fair, they were a nice bunch of lads. They told us they had been trying to get a gig at *The Cavern* for ages, without any luck, and they wished us well.

We did our bit, putting everything into it, Roy, Jeff and me playing 'In The Hall Of The Mountain King', guitars and bass behind our heads! That really impressed them, and we ended up having a very good night. We met up with Bob at *The Cavern* the next afternoon. Apparently, he had sent someone down to the pub the previous evening to see what we were like, and whoever it was had given him a glowing report.

'You're playing the lunchtime session here at *The Cavern* on Monday and I've got you another gig tonight,' proclaimed Bob.

We'd done it! On Monday, 29th June 1964, we would be playing *The Cavern*!

— CHAPTER SEVEN —

Bust Up at The Cavern

There had always been some friction between the drummer, Dave, and me. It started after a row we had one night. We were all packed into the van, coming back from a gig in Cardiff. Dave owned the van and he was the only one who could officially drive. I cannot remember what we were arguing about, but whatever it was, as we were travelling through the village of Ystrad Mynach, he snapped, pulling to the side of the road and shouting, 'Fuck off out of the van and take your gear with you!'

Ken and I unloaded my equipment from the van. There was the amp head, the bass cabinet and my bass guitar, which was now the big Fender Precision bass. I didn't know how we were going to get home carrying it all. But we didn't have a choice, because before slamming the doors Ken and I shouted in unison, 'Fuck you and fuck the group!' and Dave sped off into the night.

Carrying the speaker between us, with the guitar case on top of the speaker and the amp head on top of that, we trekked the two and a half miles to Nelson, up Tredomen Hill. Anyone from the area will know it is a steep hill. It took us hours, as we were stopping to rest every fifty yards or so, and to make matters worse, it had started to rain. On the way, Ken and I agreed we were going to form our own band.

However, we did not have time, because a few days later, there was a knock at my door. Roy was standing there with his father. He had come to ask me to re-join the group and said he and Jeff had decided that if I came back, they would get rid of Dave the drummer.

I eventually agreed on the understanding that Ken could also re-join the group. So the agreement was: we would come back and the drummer would go. However, after thinking about it overnight I realised that we were not going to get a drummer, locally anyway, anywhere near as good as Dave. There were plenty around but he was the best. We had our disagreements, but if we were to carry on with the same sound, we needed him. I asked Roy and Jeff if they would re-consider and let him stay. Whatever he had done, we were a tight-knit band, and I wanted to keep it that way. They both agreed, but Ken stipulated that Dave had to apologise, otherwise he would get a good hammering. Dave did apologise to both of us. He had to, otherwise Ken would have kept his promise!

We had been to *The Cavern* twice already, and of course we had all seen pictures of the place, but when we returned to the club on the date of our show, I realised that in our previous visits, I hadn't really had chance to take things in. It was strange seeing the club empty, but otherwise it was exactly as I had imagined it to be. I spent time looking around to take it all in: the alcove where Cilla Black used to take the coats, the narrow steps down which *The Beatles* had walked so many times… It smelt like a cross between a church and a railway station – a musty, stale sort of aroma.

I know that sounds odd, but that is the only way I can describe it. To me, the stage area had a different kind of smell; it was a more of a woody, sort of warm feeling. It gave me goosebumps. Did the young people who would shortly be dancing their lunch hour away realise that they would be dancing in the most famous club in the world? Or did they take it all for granted? People from all over the world were trying to make it to Liverpool, just to see *The Cavern* (they still are today, well the new *Cavern*) and these locals were here every day not batting an eyelid.

Then there was Bob Wooler. Bob was practically as famous as *The Cavern* itself, a friend to all the groups, and now he was taking us under his wing. Bob informed us that *The Cavern* in the late fifties was a jazz club and only started booking pop groups in 1961. I could imagine it as a jazz cellar, cigarette smoke swirling around the arches, which ran down each side of the narrow, long room; the musicians' instruments glinting in the shadow. It would have been like something from the American Deep South.

I had sang at the birthplace of rock 'n' roll and now I was standing on the same stage where just a short time ago *The Beatles* had stood, not to mention Cilla Black, *The Big Three*, *The Mersybeats*, *Gerry And The Pacemakers*, *The Swinging Blue Jeans*, Billy J Kramer, and *The Hollies*. I don't know if it was just my imagination, but the stage area under the arch did have an atmosphere all of its own. I looked around and thought of all the singers and bands that had performed there and touched one of the cold stone arches.

I was brought back to earth by Jeff's voice bellowing, 'It looks like a fucking tube station!'

Then the crowd started to arrive. I saw girls heading straight toward the front, some tucking into their sandwiches; after all, it was lunchtime. It was strange seeing them eating their lunch while we were preparing to play. We were more used to pints. But whatever our crowd's choice of sustenance, it was time for us to play our set. Bob told us to get ready to go on and to relax and enjoy the moment.

Looking out now from the stage it looked a different club. It was packed; a sea of faces gazed back at us. But would they like us? We were foreigners to them. They were used to their own home grown bands, with one or two exceptions from Manchester. No time to worry about that now. It was show time. But a second or so before Bob was to announce us, I noticed that my microphone had been changed. I looked around and saw that Dave the drummer had switched mine and his. Dave did sing a little, as did Jeff on certain songs, but the main vocals came from Roy, Ken and me. That's why we had the better quality microphones. The other two microphones were of a lower standard.

As I went over to confront Dave and to take my mic back, Bob announced us, 'Here's a great group all the way from South Wales, with a different sound, a sound of their own.'

As he was saying this, I was pulling at Dave's microphone stand. But before I could get the microphone free, Dave grabbed it, shouting, 'Fuck off, it's mine!'

'It's mine, you fucking arsehole!' I replied.

We were now both trying to wrestle the mic from each other, which was now out of the mic stand and in Dave's hands. The stand was now lying flat on the floor. I caught hold of the lead and was about to wrap it around Dave's neck when Ken stepped in, drawing back his fist. I came to my senses. 'Leave it!' I shouted. 'Let him have it. I'll use his.' By this time the crowd thought we were a comedy band. Most of them at the front were laughing their heads off, but a few were cringing at our language. I looked around at Bob and was glad to see he was laughing, but Roy had a look across his face that said, *Why are you doing this now?* We had waited so long for this moment; why did Dave go and swap the mics? He knew it would cause trouble.

Roy started blasting out on the guitar and we had to follow. We started by playing an old American rock song, putting our own twist on it. Other bands at the time were merely copying each other. As we played, I looked out at the faces of the crowd. They looked bemused. I do not believe they had heard a sound like ours before. Or maybe they had not seen anyone fighting on stage. After we finished the number, I thought it might be our last. We had hardly any response, except from a few of the girls at the front. We had been announced as a Welsh group, totally alien to them, and with our own sound, our first number had flopped. And the second number didn't do much better. Jeff turned to me and said, 'This is going well. Let's do some real obscure numbers. That'll make them choke on their fucking sandwiches.'

Ken was announcing the third number, saying that we had arranged it just for them at *The Cavern*, and that if they didn't like it, we'd stop all of them coming to Rhyl and Prestatyn for their holidays. Thousands of Liverpudlians made for the seaside towns of north Wales for their summer holidays. It was practically on their doorstep. This did the trick; they were used to banter from the local bands and Ken had sussed it. By the fourth number they were starting to warm to us, and with a bit more chat from Ken, by the end of the fifth, we had won them over. The place was buzzing. I looked over at Bob Wooler and his face was beaming. A few of the girls were writing on slips of paper, some suggesting songs, others writing what we presumed to be their name and numbers on them. I can remember the smell of their perfume wafting up and mingling with the odour of the club and the stage area. I looked around and even Dave the drummer was smiling. *The Cavern* had come alive and I realised just why so many of my heroes had come here to play. The atmosphere was electric; I had never experienced anything like it, especially in the afternoon. Some of the girls were dancing while still eating their sandwiches, and as we finished our set they screamed and cheered. I don't know about the boys. I wasn't looking at them.

Then the club was empty again. We were left with a pile of addresses and the telephone numbers from the girls, written on paper bags, tickets, and even sections of toilet paper. Last to leave was a girl who had been chatting to Ken. As she hurried across the dance floor, obviously late back to the office, I heard her shout back to him in her Liverpool accent, 'Don't forget tomorrow.'

Bob said to us afterwards that he thought we might struggle a bit, not being from the area, but he had been amazed by the reception we had received. He was also raving about the sound we produced. I couldn't believe it! Both the crowd and the manager: we had conquered *The Cavern*!

*

Some big name in the business wanted to hear us play, so Bob wrote a letter to the *Orrell Park Ballroom*, where we did a free show for the bigwig to see us, after which the offers of work began flooding in. By this time, Dave the drummer had apologised once again. He said that he had just wanted to be heard at *The Cavern*, and because I had a more powerful voice than he did, he had thought it would be all right if he swapped the microphones around. With everything going as it was, we were hardly going to hold it against him. With a prescription for penicillin from a local doctor, my throat had got better, and there was nothing standing in our way.

Things were now beginning to happen for us. We played *The Cavern* again and the girls were even more vocal than before. After the session we began getting the offers. Some wanted to know where we were playing in the evenings, saying they would come and support us. They told us that every group they had supported had become famous. Jeff came out with a classic, asking one girl if she or her mother could cook. 'Yes,' came the reply.

'Let's go back to your place then. I'm starving.'

Bob booked other slots for us and we were rolling. We filmed an advert for Lyon's Ice Cream outside the club, and there was talk of me appearing in *Ferry 'Cross the Mersey*, a film featuring *Gerry and The Pacemakers*, but that didn't go down very well with the rest of the group. Someone involved in the production had approached me at *The Cavern*. He said they were urgently looking for someone to play a part in the film; he had watched me playing with the band and thought I would be perfect for the role. But the rest of the group were worried that being offered this part just after doing the

Lyon's Ice Cream advert would whet my appetite: that I would get the acting bug and knock the band on the head. I wanted to accept the part, but it was not to be. Things were happening for us. We were all on a high and I was not going to be the one to let them down. However, the one thing that *was* letting us down was the money. We were well-known back home and on a good earner as we lived with our parents. Here in Liverpool, although we were becoming known and earning reasonable money, we had to pay to live: accommodation, food, petrol and the upkeep of the van was taking its toll, but we were surviving.

A while later we returned home for some bookings. We were only home for the Saturday and Sunday night but the two clubs we played at were packed out. Moreover, we were being mobbed wherever we went. Our fame was spreading across south east Wales, and people had now come to associate us with Liverpool and *The Cavern*. But though we had agreed to return to Liverpool at the end of the week – Ken and Dave wanted to get back as soon as possible – Roy and Jeff and I wanted to try London. What more could we achieve in Liverpool? We had played most of the top venues there and it would only be a matter of repeating the process. There were no top recording studios in Liverpool; they were all in London. All the Liverpool groups had to venture to London in the end. I desperately wanted to get back to the big city, even if it was only to play the *2i's* again. There was another group argument, and Ken and Dave were out-voted three to two, but they both suggested that we should first stay in Wales for a while to build up some money for the trip. I knew if we stayed at home, it would never happen:

we would not build up any money; Ken spent it as fast as he earned it and so did I. So I put my foot down: it was to be London, and we were to leave the next day, the 6th July 1964.

— CHAPTER EIGHT —

Tolmer Square

Roy was the last one to be picked up. As I watched him walk up his garden path towards the van, I couldn't believe my eyes. He was carrying a big stuffed owl in a glass case. He said we could sell it if we got hungry! The journey seemed to take forever in that old Thames Van; there were no motorways from South Wales to London in 1964, and we would stop every few hours at one of the transport cafés that were scattered along the A40.

Eventually, at 5.30pm, we arrived in London. We had no idea where we were going; we were completely lost, just driving around aimlessly; we hadn't even brought a map with us. In the distance, we saw a huge crowd had gathered and was blocking the road ahead. 'Our fame must be spreading,' Jeff remarked. 'They even know about us up here.' We stopped and asked a young girl where we were. She told us we were heading into Piccadilly Circus. Ken asked if there would be any animals there – the girl couldn't understand him.

'If it's a circus there will be animals there, won't there?' explained Ken.

The girl replied, 'No, but in a half an hour there will be some insects arriving.'

She told us that at 6.00pm *The Beatles* would be at the

nearby *London Pavilion* for the premier of their film *A Hard Day's Night*.

'Bollocks, drive on,' Ken said to Dave. 'Who the fuck do they think they are!'

I told Dave to turn around. It was stupid trying to get through, but he took no notice of me. He was listening to Ken shouting, 'Drive on!'

Some of the crowd thought *The Beatles* were in the back, that they were being driven to the premier in an old van as a joke. They were letting us through but were banging on the sides of the van shouting, 'Are they in the back?' We were surrounded. They were trying to open the back doors. The van was shaking. It was getting too much, so Ken shouted, 'Back up, we'll get lynched.'

At first, we could not budge. There were too many people surrounding the van, so I told Roy and Jeff to get up front and show themselves through the window to prove that there were no members of *The Beatles* in the van. This seemed to do the trick. I could hear some of the crowd yelling, 'It's not them.' The banging on the van died down and the crowd started to fall back, so slowly Dave reversed. We finally managed to turn around and get out of there, and I could see the relief on Roy, Jeff and Dave's faces. Ken was still mumbling something about, 'Who do they think they are?'

So we were back to driving around aimlessly, not really knowing where we were going, hoping to see something we recognised. Half an hour or so later, we were driving up Tottenham Court Road towards Euston Road, when all of a sudden Dave swerved to avoid a pedestrian running across the road. Unfortunately, in doing so, he hit a car that was travelling along side of us. I was in the passenger seat at the time (there was only one passenger seat at the front of the van as the engine was situated in the centre front, separating the driver and passenger). He had hit the car on my side. I looked out of the window and saw there were four or five blokes in the car. And they did not look very happy. 'Put your foot down!' I shouted. 'There's a gang in the car you just hit, Dave.'

He slammed his foot down, but the car followed. We managed to keep ahead, slipping between buses as we sped for the junction with Euston Road. I will say two good things about Dave: as well as being a great drummer, he was also an excellent driver. As we approached the junction, they were well behind; they seemed to be in a jam behind the buses. I told Dave to carry on straight ahead across the junction, whilst the rest of the boys kept a look out. The blokes in the car chasing us would not know if we had gone left, right or straight across at the junction; they were still stuck behind the traffic. Dave managed to drive straight through at the junction, and on reaching Hampstead Road, I shouted, 'Turn right,' which he did, and we entered Tolmer Square.

Turn right: those two little words were to change my life.

As we turned into the square, the first thing we saw was the *Tolmer Cinema*. It was stuck right in the middle of the square, and the road led around the cinema in a circle so you would exit the same way as you came in. There was an entry and exit for pedestrians at the back of the square, and this led to North Gower Street. Old houses that had been converted into flats surrounded the square. I found out later the cinema was formally the *Tolmer Square Congregational*

Church; it was built in 1863 and converted to a cinema in 1924. It closed on the 22nd March 1972 and with the rest of the houses was demolished and replaced with new flats. We drove around the back of the cinema and out of sight. After waiting an hour or so, and supposing it was safe, I suggested we leave the van there and head on down to Old Compton Street and the *2i's*.

As we entered the *2i's* I could see Tom Littlewood chatting to someone. I was glad he was still working there; nearly five years had gone by, but I was hoping he would still remember me. I said to the boys excitedly, 'Great, boys, Tom's still here.' We approached and I re-introduced myself: 'Hi, Tom, it's Roger, do you remember me? I was here in 1959.'

Tom stared at me dubiously, and said that if he could remember everyone who came to the *2i's* since he worked there, he'd be a bleedin' genius.

'I'm from Wales,' I replied. 'Don't you remember?'

'Don't brag about that here, son,' was his reply.

Eventually, after reminding him that it was he who had advised me back in 1959 to get myself a band, a flicker of recognition appeared in his eyes. I had followed his advice: here was my band, we were good, and we had come to crack London. I told him all about our success at *The Cavern Club* and the following we were attracting.

'Makes no difference down here. They couldn't care less whether you played *The Cavern* or not. If you had a hit record under your belt, that would be different, but again, if you had had a hit record you wouldn't be playing here, would you?'

I suppose he was right, Tom had a way with words...

sometimes. He told us he could give us a booking but it would not be for be for at least another week or two. But he did say that we could go down and watch the group playing. The basement was just about as I remembered it, still crowded and hot; the lead singer of the band had a voice that sounded like the late comic actor Kenneth Williams – but on speed, if you can imagine that! Roy couldn't stop laughing; he set the rest of us off and in the end, we couldn't take it anymore and had to leave. Unusually there was no comment from Ken at this, mind you he had been busy eyeing up one of the girls who had been dancing next to him.

That night we slept in the van, or tried to. I slept on top of my bass cabinet, Roy propped himself in a corner, Jeff did the same, while Ken was in the passenger seat and Dave in the driver's. The idea was to change positions every night, but how long could we stick this for? The next day we were all completely knackered but that didn't stop us invading the West End. We needed to find an agent quickly and procure some work. However, that afternoon Ken wanted to show the boys the pub we had visited on our 1958 trip. Dave didn't drink much, he would just have an occasional pint or two, and Roy didn't drink at all. Ken, Jeff and myself, however, were the opposite. Jeff would sometimes sneak off stage to top up his pint. Very often, I would hear Dave shouting behind me, 'He's fucked off again. This has got to stop!' and I would look towards the bar and there would be Jeff holding up his pint of beer and smiling back. Roy was oblivious to it all. He was so loud it didn't make any difference to him – he just kept on playing.

As we sat in the pub drinking, Roy and Dave kept

nagging us to save our money for food and accommodation. They were right, of course, but at the time, we never saw it that way. And, I suppose, our decision was vindicated, because when we had finished our last drink and decided to call into the *2i's* for a coffee, we arrived at exactly the right time. Tom Littlewood walked straight over to us and asked if we still wanted a booking there. One of the groups had just cancelled the following night.

'Yes!' came the reply in unison. We drank our coffee and set straight off back to the nearest pub to celebrate.

That night, it was my turn to sleep in the passenger seat. Well, I say 'sleep'; we hardly ever slept. At the time there was a product called Glees. Glees were little packets of sweets, and the main spoken line in their adverts at the time was, 'What are Glees?' In those days, my nickname was Dan – don't ask me why – and every so often, when Roy couldn't sleep, a little voice from the back of the van would chirp out, 'What are Glees, Dan? We gave up trying to stop him, so every time Roy was awake, we all were, which was most of the night.

But I must have been able to scrape together a few minutes that night, because the following morning I was awakened by a loud knocking on the passenger window. I must have been sleeping with my head up against the window, because, as I opened my eyes, I could see a woman's face pressing against the other side of the glass. It frightened me for a few seconds, waking and seeing someone's face so close. She was talking through the glass, asking if we were a group. As *The Z Men* had been painted on the side of the van, I thought it was bloody obvious that we were a group. But she kept on: 'Who are you then? Where are you from?' she asked.

I told her the name was on the side of the van and that we were from Wales. She couldn't hear me very well with the window closed, so I lowered it and told her once more.

This woke up Ken. I heard his sleepy voice mumbling behind me: 'Fuck me, Dan's pulled already, and it's only 9.00am.'

The woman wanted to know what we were doing parked up at the rear of the cinema. I told her we had come up from Wales to work and didn't have anywhere to stay. She informed us that she lived in the Square. Her name was Irene, and she had a daughter named Mimi who was a dancer. She asked if we would like a cup of tea and something to eat. She didn't have to ask twice: Jeff was awake and getting his things together, while Roy had already opened the back door and was out in the street ready to go.

Irene and Mimi lived in a basement flat which was part of a three-story house. The flat consisted of a lounge-cum-bedroom, a small kitchen, and a bathroom, which was situated outside the flat's front door along a small corridor. Mimi was an attractive, slim, half–Asian sixteen year old, around five feet seven tall with long jet-black hair. At the age of fourteen, she had been part of a professional dancing group that had toured Sweden. However, her leg was now in plaster after a car had driven into her as she was leaving a friend's flat in Notting Hill Gate. The driver had attempted to run over her again, but was fortunately prevented from doing so by a quick-thinking motorist who saw what was happening and blocked the culprit's car; he then held the offender until the police arrived. The accident had happened in late 1963, but there had been problems with the leg healing.

Mimi's father was Ali Mohammed Abbas, a Bengali, who had separated from her mother years before. He was one of the founders of the state of Pakistan and would ultimately become the first Asian barrister to work in all courts throughout the UK. From 1945 to 1979 he lived at 33 Tavistock Square, which he re-named Pakistan House. There is now a plaque outside the building commemorating his achievements. You could say Mimi had the legal profession in her blood: on her mother Irene's side of the family, her distant grandfather was Sir Samuel Romilly – famous for being instrumental in the abolition of 'hanging, drawing and quartering'.

Irene worked as a telephonist, and always had two jobs. Usually, she would work the night shift in a top class hotel, such as Browns, then it would be home early morning for a few hours' sleep, then off again to her afternoon job, in places such as Marylebone Station. I don't know how she managed to keep going on the amount of sleep she got. On hearing all this, we were doubly grateful for our tea and toast, and we were invited to visit again.

Most dairy shops in and around London in the sixties were run by the Welsh, and in the weeks to come, we would befriend many of the owners. If we went in to buy some milk we would inevitably come away with some free cheese or pasties, whatever was on offer, and with the words 'Don't forget us when you make it!' trailing after us.

However, that morning we were still strangers to the city, short of cash, and our appetites only whetted by Irene's tea and toast. There was a café situated in North Gower Street, just near the pedestrian entrance to Tolmer Square. We waited across the road, watching for the table near the door to become available. After a short while the couple occupying the table left, and we dived in, took a chair from the table behind, and the five of us squeezed together around the small table. I remember exactly what I ordered. It was lamb chops, chips, peas and a cup of tea, followed by apple pie and custard. After we finished our meal, we sat there smoking for a while, planning our exit. We were to remain until the waitress went into the kitchen and then do a runner. We didn't have to wait long, and as soon as she disappeared we were off out of the café like lightning. But we had only gone about ten yards when Ken let out a cry, 'Fuck, I've left my fags on the table!' He headed back to the café as we shouted after him, 'Leave them, you'll get caught.' But Ken had no intention of leaving them. There were only two left in the packet and he didn't have enough money to buy any more. Of course, the inevitable happened, and he was caught. A customer must have shouted to the kitchen what had happened, and as Ken leapt in to the café, the waitress and two kitchen staff pounced on him.

We were way down the road by then and couldn't see what was going on. But before long it was obvious that Ken wouldn't be reappearing any time soon.

After around an hour, for lack of any better ideas, we headed back to Irene and Mimi's, thinking we were going to be missing a singer that evening. To our surprise, Ken was sitting there drinking a cup of tea. 'What the hell happened?' Roy enquired. Ken explained that he could have belted the kitchen staff and got away, but as there was a women present, the waitress, he didn't want her to get hurt. He just explained the situation that we were a group, we were staying just around the corner in our van in Tolmer Square, we were skint and hungry, but would be playing the *2i's* that night – could we pay them for the meals the following morning? They could have called the police, but then they definitely wouldn't have got any money – we had none to give – so they decided to trust Ken. I'm happy to say that we paid them the next day, apologised, got to know the staff, and when we could afford it, would eat there again, though on our wages that wasn't that often.

Our equipment had been set up early for our first show at the *2i's*, although Tom Littlewood made the fatal mistake of telling to us that we could play as loud as we liked. The manager of the *Memo* in Barry, south Wales, to his regret, had told us the same a few months previously; we practically blew the roof off the place! We asked Tom if he was sure, explaining that though it may not look like it, we had some very powerful equipment. While other bands were using Vox AC30's, Selmer, or Fender amps – which were all great by the way – Roy was using a souped-up American Ampeg guitar amp, which had a huge sound. Jeff's amp was also mega-loud, and to compete, I had a huge bass cabinet coupled with a powerful bass amp. But Tom didn't seem bothered, telling us that we couldn't possibly be louder than some of the bands that they had previously had.

So when the time came and we stood on stage looking over the crowd, Roy turned to us with a smile on his face, and said, 'OK, boys, let them have it.' We started our first number, the sound bouncing off the walls in the small cellar and booming back at us with a force that was almost physical. I looked at Roy, who's face had changed from a smile to a smirk, as if to say, *you asked for it, now you're getting it*. After a short while, someone from outside the café must have called the police, because three of them arrived, shouldering their way through the crowd, to tell us to turn the volume down. Tom Littlewood said afterwards that the music was coming up through the vents in the pavement, and that outside there had been people dancing along the street. He was having a good giggle about that. He proceeded to say that he had let us play for a while because he thought it was a good sound, and was about to tell us to turn down but the police had beaten him to it.

The next morning Irene invited us to her flat again for a cup of tea and a bite to eat with her and Mimi. Mimi's real name was Naseema. Her mother had nicknamed her Mimi after a character from a film and because she thought it would be a good showbiz name for her. I think, at the time, we all fancied Mimi, but our only thought was how to get the group established. Nothing was going to deter us from that, or so we thought.

That afternoon we headed back to the *2i's* to speak with Tom Littlewood. He informed us that he had received some great reports from the regulars about our performance and wanted to line up some more bookings for us. Also, someone had approached him and asked for our telephone number. Tom had no idea how to contact us so he had taken his business card. We were beginning to find that not having a phone number was making things difficult (there were no mobile phones in those days). Tom said he would start to line up some work for us, so the next time we saw Irene and Mimi we asked if they might take phone messages for us, and they kindly agreed.

The next day we rang the number on the business card and some bloke answered; he didn't tell me his name so I didn't ask. He said he was working for agent and show presenter Roy Tempest. He asked if we would do an audition at a small club in the West End. The audition went well and Roy Tempest thought we were great (his words). He told us he organised tours for big-name artistes and booked many of the clubs around London. He also mentioned that he was from Cardiff and invited us to his apartment the next night to talk business.

The next evening we arrived at Roy's apartment full of anticipation. On stepping inside, Jeff remarked, 'Bloody hell! This is something else!' To us it was like walking on to a film set. I suppose we shouldn't have been surprised that it was very luxurious, but one thing I don't think any of us could have expected was the live leopard wandering about. It looked like a baby, but in later days Roy, our guitarist, swore that it was a fully grown tiger.

Roy Tempest said that we had impressed him at the audition, and he could, if we wanted, organise some work, probably a tour for us, and again, if it was agreeable, try to procure us a recording deal. We jumped at the chance; we would have regular work and a chance of maybe finding a flat. I'm not sure we even processed the potential for a recording deal; at the time, it was the last thing on our minds.

Around this time, the name of our group changed from *The Z Men* to the *The Pitmen*. Later, we would always disagree over who changed the name. I maintain it was Tom Littlewood. I remember him saying that, us being from Wales, where there were so many pits (mines), the name would give us an edge. But Roy and Jeff thought it was Roy Tempest, while Ken would say he couldn't give a fuck and that we could always change it back. Ken always had a way with words!

Our first booking outside London was at *Godalming Blues Club*, Surrey. I am vague as to who booked us there, but whoever it was had asked us if we could do a few numbers backing an American soul artiste by the name of Sonny Charles. We found out later that he usually worked with his own band, but for some reason, that night he was on his own, so he might have been promoting a solo record.

We arrived at the club early to set up our equipment. There was no sign of Sonny Charles, so off we went to find a local pub. We arrived back at the venue early to make sure everything was in working order. We had already done a sound check, but we always made sure, just in case someone had tampered with our guitars. We picked up our instruments to make sure they were in tune, and Roy went to town blasting out a blues number. He was still playing when this guy, who I instantly recognised as Brian Jones from *The Rolling Stones*, came walking up to us accompanied by two other blokes, who I assumed were his minders. 'What the hell is he doing here?' Ken bellowed over the noise.

'That was great, man,' commented Brian, once Roy had finished.

Roy had his back to him and replied, grimacing, 'I'm just tuning up.'

He wasn't usually abrupt with people, but on this occasion he wanted to make sure everything was spot on, and Brian Jones had interrupted his procedure.

Brian replied, 'OK, might see you later. I've just come in to see Sonny Charles. We've played here in the past. It's a good club. Have a great night.'

Then he'd gone, wandering off to the dressing room to find Sonny. Roy noodled away, oblivious of who he had just spoken to. When Sonny arrived we did a quick rehearsal with him, running through the two blues numbers he was planning to do. I still cannot understand why he was performing just two numbers that evening, unless it was for Brian Jones. But the music was just our cup of tea! Our first spot went very well and halfway through the second spot we introduced Sonny, who nailed it. He had a great voice. It was the first official blues club that we had ever played; we had a great reception from the crowd and we loved every minute of it.

The bookings were coming in at a steady pace, so we decided to find ourselves a flat. A letting agency came up with one in Westbourne Park Road, Bayswater. It was on the first floor, cheap and basic, and we only had to pay a week's rent in advance. There was only one problem: it only had two beds, so we took it in turn to use them.

London in those days, I would say, was just as exciting as it had been on my first visit in 1958, but the music scene had definitely changed. While in the past it had been a Mecca for solo performers – Cliff Richard, Marty Wilde, et al. – now it was all groups, or lead singers with their own group. Compared to the few Rock 'n' Rollers of the mid to late '50s, there were hundreds, even thousands of them. They came from all over the country; everyone now wanted to get to London.

There was a pub in Old Compton street that had a jukebox and for a shilling it would play a film of the artiste whose record was playing. The lip-sync was spot on; this was unique in 1964. I vividly remember watching Screaming Lord Sutch singing 'Jack The Ripper', and also *Johnny Kidd and The Pirates* singing 'Shakin' All Over', and being amazed.

There were still some clip joints around. These were small clubs and bars, mostly situated in basements around Dean Street, Old Compton Street, and other parts of Soho, which employed glamorous-looking girls to hook up with male visitors. The girls would encourage their unsuspecting victims to take them down into the clubs, where sometimes there would be a sex show on for extra incentive. Once in, the girls would ply the men with watered-down drinks, or even coloured water claiming to be champagne. After he had been there a while, he would be presented with an extortionate bill, and if he refused to pay or didn't have enough money on him, a bouncer would be sent over to take what he had.

The coffee bars were on the decline but there were still a few hanging on. The *2i's* was still booking groups, while *Le Macabre* coffee bar, situated in Meard Street off Wardour Street, had carved out its own odd little niche. It had black walls, the tables were coffins, and Bakelite skulls were used as ashtrays; the lights were in plastic skulls and there were skeletons hanging from the walls. One evening I met Screaming Lord Sutch there and he didn't look out of place. He would usually appear in his top hat and cape, sometimes with what appeared to be blood running down his whitened face. This was highlighted by his long black hair. In his performances, he would constantly scream at the girls in order to frighten them. It would all seem very tame by today's standard, but back then he was unique, and some of the young girls were genuinely terrified of him. David Sutch, which was Screaming Lord Sutch's real name, would eventually, in 1983, form The Monster Raving Loony Party and stand in numerous parliamentary elections.

The main venues at the time were *The Crawdaddy Club* at the back of *The Railway Hotel* in Richmond, Surrey; the hotel on Eel Pie Island, an island in the middle of the Thames; also *Godalming Blues Club*; *100 Club*, Oxford Street; *The Marquee Club*, Wardour Street; *The Flamingo*, Wardour street; and *Tiles*, Oxford Street. On any given night you could stop in and catch the likes of *The Rolling Stones, Manfred Mann,* Georgie Fame, *The Nashville Teens, Pretty Things, The High Numbers* (soon to become *The Who*), *The Kinks*, and many more.

The bookings were coming in, but the money was not enough to live on. We needed to up our prices. We were eating peas on toast every meal – that's all we could afford. Peas were much cheaper than beans, and I became addicted to them. I remember one day at the flat we all clubbed together, bought some bread, butter, and cheese, and made Welsh rarebit (cheese on toast). It was as good as a feast. Satisfied, Ken, Roy, Jeff, and I went over the pub for a drink, leaving Dave behind and a small amount of cheese on the shelf (we did not have a fridge). After a pint each and a Coke for Roy, we returned, and Ken noticed the cheese was missing. Dave's suggested that the mice must have eaten it.

'Funny mice,' replied Ken. 'They must have screwed up the wrapping paper and put it in the bin.' Ken went berserk, though not before Dave had made a quick exit out to the van, drove to Mimi's flat, and begged sanctuary by telling her we were going to beat him up. In the end there was, yet again, another apology from Dave. Meanwhile Roy's parents came to the rescue, paying us a flying visit, driving up from Wales and bringing with them boxes of food, coffee, and tea. Ken said it would be great if they could make it a weekly occurrence.

One evening, Mimi introduced us to her friend Rose. She was from Hammersmith, and all she could talk about was the men she had dated – her conquests! Ken fancied her like mad. So when we managed to get a booking at an American air base, somewhere between Cambridge and Norwich, Ken wanted to take Rose and Mimi along. Mimi wasn't too sure because she was still in some pain with her leg, but reluctantly agreed.

The Americans really took to us. We were playing their kind of music! If they requested a song and we played it, they plied us with drink. If they requested a song and we didn't know it, they still plied us with drink. We could do no wrong in their eyes. We were on with a group called *The Honeycombs*. Roy and Ken didn't like them but Jeff and I were impressed. They were playing out-and-out-pop music, had a distinctive sound, a female drummer and a great lead vocalist. When the night ended, I went over to speak to two of the boys. After a general chitchat, they told me how their record producer, Joe Meek, was going to get them to number one. They had released a record in June and it was slowly starting to sell. I had never heard of Joe Meek, but I *had* heard both of the number one hits he had produced. In 1962 he had written and produced 'Telstar' for *The Tornados*, which had reached number one in the USA. And in 1961, he had produced John Leyton's hit 'Johnny, Remember Me', written by Geoff Goddard. The boys explained Meek was a recording pioneer, that he was touched by genius. They told me I should go and see him, and said that I could be a pop star in my own right. I explained to them that I only sang a few songs, and that I mainly sang backing vocals. They said, 'We know, we've just been listening to you. You should concentrate on becoming a singer in your own right. Go and see him.' They gave me the telephone number of his studio in Holloway Road. I thanked them, we said our goodbyes, and I headed back to the boys for a last drink before we left.

— CHAPTER NINE —

Goodbye to The Z Men

It was a Thursday and we were returning to Wales to fulfil a Friday and Saturday booking. We thought it would be a good idea to travel home a day early and have a night out. We were the homecoming heroes, London up-and-comers back for a victory lap. But the boys kept asking me what was wrong. They said I looked as if I was in a daze. And they were right. I couldn't stop thinking about that chat with *The Honeycombs*. Should I ring Joe Meek?

Back home I tried to put it to the back of my mind, taking the opportunity to catch up with some old friends. My sister Cheryl was glad to see me and said, 'At least you're not going to run away this time!'

We did our Friday booking and had a ball. There were many familiar faces in the crowd, and we lapped up the attention. The Saturday booking was even better. We were playing the Institute at Cwmfelinfach near Blackwood, a local venue for us, and we tore the place apart.

But the next day we were in for a shock. Jeff had decided not to return to London. He said that he'd had enough. I was surprised and upset, as were the others. Jeff was a good rhythm guitarist; he really filled out the sound. He played a type of rhythm mixed with bass that blended well with my own playing. He could also play lead guitar. Not only that, we were close: he was a good drinking buddy of mine, a good laugh and a good friend. I had always thought that Roy would be the first to leave. His parents never liked the idea of us struggling in London. My parents felt the same. They couldn't understand why we would choose to live in poverty when we could be earning top money in Wales, but they never tried to persuade me not to go back. They knew I loved working London, especially in the West End. There was an excitement there in those days that you couldn't find anywhere else, and we were slowly making a name for ourselves.

On the Monday we headed back to London without Jeff. There was a sombre mood in the van. We had to pass the Institute where we had played the previous evening, and just as we were approaching it, a car on the opposite side of the road swerved out. Dave veered to his right to avoid it and smashed into the wall of the Institute. I had been sat in the passenger seat and was thrown forward, bouncing off the engine cover. Dave was propelled into the side pillar of the van (there were no seatbelts in those days). Roy and Ken, along with the equipment, were smashed into the front seats, with the two of them hurtling over the top and landing on top of me, followed by a few amplifier heads.

Good fortune must have been with us that day, because none of us were seriously hurt. But the van wasn't so lucky: the front was very badly damaged, probably beyond repair. There was no way we could afford to buy another van, so that was it, the end of the dream. Before the van was towed away, we took our equipment out of it, with friends and family arriving to help us home. In the days that followed, I felt so down. Don't get me wrong, it was nice to be home, but I was missing the excitement of the big city. Eventually I began looking for work, trying to find a group that needed a bass player/singer. I didn't have to look for long. One morning, unexpectedly, a van pulled up outside my parent's house. It was Dave. His father had managed to get the vehicle repaired. This was fantastic news! I know we'd had our differences in the past but, when the chips were down, Dave had come up trumps. However, would Roy return to London after all that had happened? He'd had time at home and both Dave and I were doubtful. Not so with Ken – he was raring to go. But I should not have doubted Roy. When asked, his answer was 'When do we leave?' In fact, we left two days later.

On our return to London Tom Littlewood put a songwriter in touch with us. I cannot remember his name. He hired a place in the West End (it looked like an old church hall) and wanted us to rehearse some of the songs he had written. He played us the first one, a catchy number. I would call it a *Searcher's* type song. We got the chord structure and the songwriter seemed to like the sound we produced. The second song was even better and I would say, it could well have been a number one, but I could see Roy was not a happy chappy. He liked rock and blues music – this was not his cup of tea.

Three or four hours later, after rehearsing a few more songs, he took me aside and said, 'That's it, I've had enough! This isn't our type of music. It's good but not us.'

I had to tell the songwriter, 'Sorry, mate, but the lead guitarist won't play this type of music. Do you have any rock or blues numbers?'

'No! Why didn't you tell me in the first place that you didn't like my songs?' he asked, and stormed off in a huff.

'But we do like the songs, it's just not for us.' I yelled back, but it was too late, he didn't hear me, he was gone. When Tom Littlewood heard about it, he was not at all pleased – in fact, he was fuming.

That night we went to see *The High Numbers* play. They were later to become *The Who*, and they were playing a club where in a few night's time we would also be appearing. Roy liked them. He liked the way Pete Townsend de-tuned his guitar while playing the lead break, and he and Pete got on like a house on fire. I didn't think too much of them at the time, but I did like the bass player. Pete Townsend turned up at our booking and he was fascinated by Roy's guitar tuning, which was an open tuning. He couldn't understand how Roy had made up his own chords to that tuning; he said it was unique. It was a great night for us and we equalled, if not bettered, *The High Numbers'* response. Some of the crowd even said that they had seen virtually every band in London, and we had the best sound they had heard. That was a great compliment for us.

The next morning, Ken looked out of the window just in time to see the landlord and one of his heavies getting out of a car.

Ken woke us, shouting, 'The fucking landlord's on his way up!' He had been round once before, hassling us for some rent. As we had rented the flat through an agency, we had previously told him that we would pay up the arrears to them. We had perhaps, shall we say, been remiss in doing so...

We always unloaded our equipment at night and kept

it in the flat. It was a hassle, but we knew it would be safe. 'Stack it up against the door!' Ken shouted, so we did.

Just as we finished piling up the equipment, there was a loud knock at the door, then another, even louder, knock. We could hear a key being inserted. We had our backs against the speakers forcing them against the door, all except Roy, who was sitting on the floor with his feet against them. We were all dead quiet as the landlord fiddled with the key, evidently unable to understand why the door wouldn't open.

'They must be in there,' we heard his henchman say.

The landlord shouted, 'We know you're in there. Open the door!' We sat in dead silence. At the time, we owed the agency over three weeks rent, but we didn't have the money to pay – we were totally skint! They began trying to bust the door open, we presumed with their shoulders. He shouted again: 'We know you're there, open up!' Complete silence. Then, again, still more angrily: 'We know you're in there!'

'No we're not, fuck off!' Ken shouted back.

'What did you say that for?' Dave hissed.

'Fuck them,' said Ken, hauling the speakers down. He ripped open the door and shouted, 'Right! Who's fucking first? Fuck that, I'll take both of you together, you pair of c***s!' We knew Ken wouldn't be backing down now, so we piled out into the hallway after him, shouting and raving. The landlord was a weedy little bastard, but his henchman looked as if he could handle himself, and I was glad to see him back off.

On their way down the stairs, the landlord shouted back at us, 'We'll be back. You won't get away. We know every area of London, you bunch of wankers!'

Ken shouted back, 'You got the last part right!'

We loaded our equipment back in the van and hightailed it as fast as we could back to the West End. That afternoon we went to see Tom Littlewood at the *2i's*, but was told he wouldn't be in until early evening.

As we sat and waited, I spotted Gordon Mills and Tommy Scott (the future Tom Jones). The last time I had seen Tommy was back in Wales, when I was playing with *The Vampires*. He had come over to Blackwood from Pontypridd with a mate. Tommy, in those days, liked a good drink. We often shared a pint together and, on many occasions, he would get on stage and sing. Years later, after he had become successful, *The Greyhound* pub in Llanfabon near Pontypridd still had a large photograph of him from those days on the wall of the bar. It had been taken before he'd had an operation to alter his nose. Despite Tom asking the landlord to take it down, he never did.

After a few more pints Tommy said, 'C'mon, let's go to *The Stute*. We'll get in free. I went down well there last week.'

But he was wrong! We still had to pay two shillings. We watched the band and I introduced him to some of the boys, but after around an hour or so I could see he was getting fed up, so we headed to *The Red Lion*, where we just sat and talked about music. I had seen Tommy with Gordon (who was Tommy's manager) quite a few times around the West End. He would usually be sat in a car waiting for Gordon, who was always off doing a deal somewhere. I always stopped and chatted, asking how he was getting on in the big city, but I never once saw his group with him. I learned later that they were back at their flat in Lime Grove practically starving.

That afternoon, Tommy had a problem, Gordon told me there was another Tommy Scott on the scene – a songwriter who also did a bit of singing – and people in the industry were getting confused with the two. Gordon said he had decided on a name change. I nodded; we already knew about Tommy Scott the songwriter, as we had met him briefly in an agent's office.

'So, where are you off now?' asked Tommy.

'Going to see the Albert Finney film *Tom Jones* before our booking tonight,' I replied.

Roy chirped up and said, 'That's a great name for you Tommy, especially coming from Wales.'

Gordon instantly replied, 'That is his real name: Thomas Jones Woodward.'

'Bollocks,' Ken replied. 'Who'd have a surname like Jones for a middle name?'

'I'm telling you it is!' replied Gordon.

Not so: Tommy's real name is Thomas John Woodward. For a long time, the rumour was that Jimmy Savile had thought up the name 'Tom Jones'. And an executive from Decca records once told me *he* had named him. 'This is all bollocks!' as Ken would say! We (well, mainly Roy) christened Tom Jones that afternoon in the *2i's* coffee bar.

I would not see Gordon Mills again until 1969, at Janie Jones's house in Campden Hill Road, W8, and that would be a meeting I would rather forget.

The writing was on the wall and the band was now coming to its natural end. Deep down I knew we were out of control. We had had a lot of fun along the way, but we owed money for the rent, and we had the local villains on our tail. They knew the name we were working under – it was on the van! It would not be long before they caught up with us. We were earning a pittance in London, under a quarter of the amount we could earn back in Wales. We had refused the songwriter's material, which we found out later had been especially written for us. It had all been arranged for us by Roy Tempest to try to procure a recording deal. To be fair, Roy Tempest wanted to keep working us, he liked us so much. Nevertheless, reports were being sent back that we were drinking excessively on gigs. Since Jeff had left, it was only Ken and I who liked a drink; it never affected our playing ability, as we would only have a pint or two before we started. We, of course, would be the first to admit that we did like a few afterwards. However, the bookers had been told by club organisers that we were unruly and were looking for trouble. One booker had apparently warned Roy Tempest that we were a fantastic band but were trouble, and that we should be sent back to Wales to work in the mines. Even after all this, Roy Tempest still wanted to be our agent, telling us to cool it and concentrate on the music. I think deep down we couldn't have cared less if we made it or not, as long as we went well in the clubs, had a good time, and made a bit of money on top.

That evening, after the booking, we made our way back to Tolmer Square and knocked on Irene and Mimi's door. Mimi was there with a friend. We made ourselves a cup of tea and had a long talk about whether or not to go back to Liverpool, but after a long discussion, it was decided that we should head for home. At least we could earn some decent money in Wales. We talked most of the evening, eventually nodding off where we sat.

I think it must have been around 7.30am when Irene arrived home from her night job. Roy and I were awake, and Ken and Dave were sleeping. We told Irene of our decision to return to Wales. She was upset. She had come to like us, and she thought we were silly to go back now we were making a name for ourselves in London. 'Just behave, work hard, and you'll get somewhere,' she said. But I don't think anything could have changed our minds. We were what we were: a bunch of boys out for a good time. Musically, we had changed into a professional Rock/Blues outfit, but as people, we still looked and felt like rockers. More sophisticated Welsh bands were now emerging and would be successful in London; we hadn't moved with the times. But I did mention to Irene that I didn't really want to go back, and that Dave the drummer was also reluctant to return home. She said that Dave and I could stay at her flat for a while, and I knew I couldn't turn her down. I wasn't done with London yet.

So it was agreed that Dave and I would remain in London. Dave would drive Roy and Ken home and then return the following day. Mid-morning we said our goodbyes. It was a sad time for all of us. As I stood in Tolmer Square, waving them off, Ken popped his head out of the van window and shouted, 'You'll be back. You'll be back!' Dave never returned the following day or the day after. He never rang or got in touch. It would be over a year before I would see him again.

— CHAPTER TEN —

The Genius of Joe Meek

I was on my own once again in the big city. I had my bass guitar and amplifier, and a roof over my head, but for how long I didn't know. After three or four days, I began to feel I had made the wrong decision. I was feeling down and depressed. I missed the boys. I had no money and no job and was considering phoning my parents to send me money for the fare home.

I scoured the music paper ads for work and headed down to Denmark Street to try to find some contacts. I did not venture back to the *2i's*, as I didn't want Tom Littlewood to see that I was back to square one.

One afternoon, I managed to get some recording session work in a studio in Denmark Street. I spotted a group unloading musical instruments, when I asked them if they needed a bass player or singer, I received the reply, 'both.' By coincidence their bass player had just phoned the studio and was unable to make it.

We borrowed a small bass amp and a bass guitar from Selmer's (music shop) and I did the session. It was a simple twelve-bar blues number, and as well as playing the bass line, I sang a harmony with two other members of the band. I didn't even ask their name. All that interested me was the three pounds that they said they would pay me. I had played on my first record in a London recording studio and, I must admit, it did lift me.

That evening I opened my bass guitar case and took out my bass to practise. I opened the compartment where I kept the strap, and in it was the piece of paper I had taken from *The Honeycombs*. I had found Joe Meek's telephone number. I'd thought I had lost it! Maybe he could give me some work. It must be worth a try.

The following morning I rang the number and a man's voice answered, but it wasn't Joe Meek. I was told later that Joe never answered the phone unless he was expecting a call from someone important. I explained that I was looking for some work as a bass player or singer. The voice told me to hang on and that he would go and speak to Joe. I hung on, and on, and on, and on. Eventually, the voice returned: 'Hello, mate, sorry about that. I had to help Joe with something. He's busy at the moment, mate. Can you ring back in a couple of days?' I told him I would, but just as I was going to put the phone down, I could hear a voice in the background.

'Hang on,' said the voice on the line. 'Joe just asked if you can play guitar as well as bass.'

'I can play rhythm,' I said. 'I'm not too hot on lead.'

I could hear a voice mumbling, somewhere in the background again, and then there was another question, 'Can you sing harmonies?'

I told him I could.

'Joe says to get over here by 12.30.'

'Where are you?' I asked.

'304 Holloway Road,' he replied.

Where is Holloway? I thought. Mimi wasn't around, so I

phoned Irene at her work for directions.

The studio was a hundred or so yards from Holloway tube station. When I arrived, I was expecting a really state-of-the-art studio. After all, 'Telstar' had been a number one hit all over the world! This was just a three-storey flat up above a leather shop. The guy who I had spoken to on the phone greeted me. I followed him up the stairs, to the second floor. It didn't look much better than the flat where we had lived in Westbourne Park Road. I remember thinking it was grubby: lots of tape boxes, papers and tape reels strewn everywhere. It smelled musty. Doors were propped open and thick cables were blocking the doorways. There was a bathroom, control room and a larger front room on the floor. The control room to the left was full of racks and equipment covered with dials, switches, sliders and other mysterious gizmos. There were tables buckling with tape recorders and bits of tape everywhere, including the floor. It looked a complete mess. I couldn't believe I was in the recording studio of probably the most inventive, pioneering British record producer of all time. It was a shambles.

As I edged into the room, Joe – I assumed it was Joe; he looked in charge – turned to face me, blurting out, 'I've just been bouncing a track across, so you have a free track to record on, what's your name?'

'Roger,' I replied.

'Roger, Roger, Roger,' he said, with a hint of a West Country accent.

'No, there's only one of me!' came my response.

'He's quick!' said Joe, turning to the guy that had shown me in. 'I'll have to watch him. So, you're the bass player that plays guitar and sings harmonies?'

'I can sing lead voice as well,' I replied.

'Oh, we got a right little star here, haven't we?'

I emphasised once again that I could play a bit of lead but was only comfortable playing rhythm guitar and, of course, bass. Joe explained that he might need a bass player for a few sessions in the near future, and then asked where my guitar was. I told him I didn't have one. I could play guitar, but I didn't own a guitar; I was a bass player. His face changed as he turned to the other guy and snapped, 'Have we got a guitar for the guitarist?' The guy came back with slim semi-acoustic Hofner. 'Do you know how to tune it?' he said sarcastically.

'If you've got a piano,' I replied. 'Oh, and if it's in concert pitch.'

Joe wanted me to put a guitar on three numbers; he said to fill them out a bit, and that he would also be adding a special effect to the guitar afterwards. I didn't ask him what sort of effect; I didn't care; at that point in time all I cared about was getting paid. It was an easy chord structure. Joe went over and over each one with me, while I wrote the chords down. I recall he had some of the written music there but I remember telling him that it would be quicker for me if I did it my way. Joe was always on the go. He bustled in and out of the studio as I tuned, and I heard him clattering about. As he popped in and out, he asked me where I originated from and what I had been doing. When I mentioned *The Cavern* he said that he could have had *The Beatles*.

'For recording?' I asked.

'What else do you think it would be for?' I must have

hit a nerve; everyone in the music business knew Joe was gay, and I believe he thought I was taking the piss. So it wasn't a good start for me. It was a long session, with Joe adjusting the sound, then going over it again and again. He was a perfectionist, all right. He then asked me to put a simple lead part over one of the songs, which I did. I asked him who would be recording the songs I was playing on, and he seemed a bit vague, but he told me later that two were demos (demonstration discs) for future projects for *The Honeycombs* and the other for a solo artiste whose name I'm afraid I can't remember.

However, he firmly stated, 'Don't get any ideas. You're not getting royalties on these.'

I had not expected any. As far as I was concerned, I was hoping to be paid for the session and no more. I had previously listened to some of Joe's records, and was impressed by the vocal sound he achieved. I mentioned this to him after we had finished the session. He smiled and said that the sound was only possible through his own equipment and that other producers couldn't achieve that unique vocal effect. Then he snapped, 'What about the rest of the sound?'

'Oh, that's OK,' I replied.

'OK, only OK?'

'No, I mean you get a great recording sound. Some of the best sounds I have ever heard.'

'I should think so,' Joe said, his voice much calmer now. I was just about to unplug my guitar when he said, 'Just put a few chords down on this one, and a quick harmony part.' It was a whole other song and we went on working for at least another forty-five minutes. The normal session fee in those days was six pounds for three hours. I was there for over four and a half hours, but not only did Joe say he would pay me only six pounds but that he would have to owe it to me! He did say he was happy with what I had done and that he would use me in future sessions, but I had to explain to him that I was broke and needed the money. After a consultation with the other guy, I was handed a couple of pounds and a further promise of more work.

Over the years, I did a number of sessions for Joe, but it never got any easier to get any money out of him. There was always some excuse why he couldn't pay me the full amount. However, what I did get from Joe was knowledge of the recording industry, which would prove invaluable to me in the future. Joe's recording techniques were unique. Most mixing desks at the time were laid out horizontally in front of you, allowing the sliders, switches and knobs to be easily accessible whilst remaining seated. Joe's mixing desks had these big cooker-style knobs which ran vertically up the wall on metal racks, so he would be standing whilst at the controls. He had his own plate, tape, valve, and reverb echo units. Most reverb units in guitar or PA amplifiers were spring reverb units, usually consisting of a small metal oblong box, around ten or twelve inches long, with a couple of springs stretching the length inside. Sometimes, on stage, if you moved abruptly and yanked on the amplifiers, the reverb springs would clank together and make a horrific sound.

I later found out that Joe achieved some of his unique vocal sounds by using a builder's plank of wood, which was around fifteen feet or maybe longer. Bedsprings were stretched along the length of the board, with nails holding the springs taught. At one end of the board there was a box of electrics that would take a standard jack lead, then a lead that went into another box placed on the floor, and from there into his vertical mixing units on the wall. Joe was unbelievably inventive, and a true genius in the recording world.

He also had this old upright piano in the studio, which was not that wonderful for recording. Joe wanted a bright honky-tonk sound, so he pushed drawing pins into the hammers. This captured the sound, but there was a problem: when the piano was played, there would be drawing pins flying everywhere. Tin foil was becoming popular, so eventually he scrapped the drawing pins and replaced them with the aluminium foil, another inventive idea.

Joe was eccentric, all right. I popped into his studio one day to see a musician friend of mine. As we were about to leave, Joe appeared dressed in a very nice suit; it was made from a shiny mohair material and, with collar and tie, he looked very smart. However, he was also wearing his carpet slippers. He asked us to hurry up and leave, as he had a meeting to attend somewhere in the West End. As we hurried down the stairs and out of the door, with Joe rushing behind us, I turned to my musician friend and whispered, 'Shall we tell him about the slippers?'

'No, best not to,' he replied. So off went Joe to his meeting wearing his carpet slippers.

In late January 1967, I begun working on a few songs at Joe's with a guitarist from Sydenham named Barry. Barry had known Joe for some time, and had worked on many sessions for him over the years. He had written a few original numbers and roped me in to play and sing harmonies on the tracks. He also wanted me to record a song entitled 'Kentucky Woman', which had been written and recorded by Neil Diamond and was eventually released in Britain later in 1967. Barry, through his connections, had acquired a copy of the song before its release date. He thought it suited my voice, and wanted me to record it. His idea was to have one of his original songs as the A-side and put me on the B-side – that way we would have two chances to get airplay. If the record companies weren't too keen on his original song, we might get a release on the Neil Diamond number. In those days the B-side would earn 50% of the single so Barry wasn't bothered which song became the A-side. We ran through the song at Joe's to see what he thought of it. Joe was impressed, and we did a quick demo, but for release purposes, he was only interested in recording Barry's original material. Later that day he did say that he might be interested in recording a master, but that we couldn't release it by law until the Neil Diamond version came out in Britain. I don't know if that was true or not.

But we never got a chance to record again with Joe – not the Neil Diamond number, not anything at all. On the day we were to record the master tracks of Barry's song, we turned up at the studio and were refused entry. Joe had shot and killed Mrs Shenton, the owner of the ground floor shop, and then shot himself.

Soon the police arrived and the world would shortly learn the truth. It was such a horrific end for such a talented man.

The same week as I met Joe, I bought a copy of the *Melody Maker*, the number one music paper at the time. I was scouring the adverts for work when I came across one which read: 'Bass player for a band that is under management, earning money, and going places.'

I phoned them and, when I mentioned that I had just been recording with Joe Meek, they immediately took interest. The group were from Harrogate and they were called *The Tonix*. In my stupidity, I somehow thought Harrogate was in North London. I had seen the signs for Harrow & Wealdstone and had mistakenly thought: *Harrow, Harrogate – they must be next door*. When I realised my mistake, I telephoned the group back and told them I would be there in three day's time, if that was OK with them. I had to try and get some cash together for the train fare and to buy some new clothes. Luckily, Irene loaned me the money. The clothes came from a guy we had met in the West End on a couple of occasions. He went by the name of Fee-fee. They had named him Fee-fee because, in cockney terms, he was a feef (thief). I desperately needed a suit, shirts, shoes and jeans. I wanted to look the part. I had been left with only two old pairs of jeans, a shirt, a tee shirt, a coat, pair of shoes and a spare polo-neck jumper.

I scoured the West End for Fee-fee, asking in different clip-joints and coffee bars if anyone had seen him, but no one would give me any information. In Fee-fee's profession, it didn't do for your whereabouts to be public knowledge! He was the best in the business and the police had never caught up with him. Eventually, I spotted him coming out of the basement of a well-known clip-joint. When I explained what I wanted from him, and told him the reason, he hesitated. It wasn't because he couldn't get the clothes. It was the fact that I couldn't pay him. With some persuasion, he eventually agreed to help me, but emphasised that if he didn't get paid and I ventured back to the West End, I would know what to expect. I agreed, and arranged to meet him later at one of the clubs. I realised it was wrong to put myself in his debt like this, but at the time, I was desperate. Right on the dot, he turned up at the meeting place, with everything I had asked for. The suit was fantastic: dark blue in colour, it must have cost a fortune. The shoes were also top quality, so were the shirts. We said our goodbyes, and early next morning I was off to Harrogate, with one case and my Fender bass and amplifier, which were put in the luggage carriage.

When I arrived at Harrogate station, Sylvia Leon, one of the two lead singers of *The Tonix*, together with the lead and rhythm guitarists, were there to greet me. Sylvia was an attractive dark-haired girl with a great voice. They had arranged for me to stay at the flat of a friend of theirs. He was working away for a few days and would be back the following week. I had arrived late Friday afternoon, and as they dropped me at the flat, I was told that I would be picked up on the Monday morning and taken to meet the other members of the band and then we would have a rehearsal. I would be on my own all over the weekend. What were they doing? Were they playing somewhere? If I was joining their band why hadn't they invited me along? Maybe they had already found a bass player locally and it was an excuse to get rid of me. I had enough money left to buy some fish and chips that evening, and there were four eggs in the fridge to last me until Monday – what a welcome! I had the phone number of the guitarist, but I thought, *No, I'll stick it out over the weekend*. But what if they didn't want me? What if they didn't like my playing? How was I going to get back?

The weekend passed slowly and, sure enough, they arrived at 10.00am on Monday. When I explained to them about not having any food, they went straight to the shops and came back with four carrier bags full. They had not been aware of my situation and they gave me an advance on my earnings. If they didn't like my playing, at least I'd have enough money to get back to London.

I need not have worried: they did like my playing, and our first rehearsal went well. They were a terrific group with a powerful sound and two great lead singers. My first baptism with the group was in a big college hall. It was a fantastic night. Then, mid-week, we played *The Cheltenham Club*, a local nightclub. The following week John, whose flat I had been staying at, returned home. He was in the insurance business and travelled all over the country. I liked him, and we seemed to get on well together. He played a bit of rhythm guitar and said he would like to join a band, but had trouble barring the chords. Barring is pressing your forefinger across the six strings of the guitar neck as part of a chord. I practised with him but he just didn't seem to get it. He told me he had a friend living somewhere near Leeds who played lead guitar for Marty Wilde's group *The Wildcats*, and said he would take me over to meet him.

On 1st September 1964 *The Yorkshire Post* wrote an article about us. This caught the eye of some showbiz bigwigs and, the following weekend, Sydney Rose came to Yorkshire to see us perform. Sydney worked for an entertainment agency in London that handled many of the stars of that era. He liked us and immediately started negotiations for our assault on London. I had only been in Yorkshire a matter of weeks and I was just getting used to living and working there, and now they wanted us to hit London. We were 'managed' – supposedly, anyway; I never signed anything – by Dennis Stephenson, assistant lecturer in Mathematics and president of the Students' Association at the college we had played. We heard through him that Sydney Rose was lining up Eric Eastman to take over as our manager. Eric Eastman had been co-manager with Andrew Loog Oldham of *The Rolling Stones*. It was all happening so fast. Sylvia, Simon and I drove down to London for the arranged meeting. On the way they filled me in on some details, and I realised what was happening. Rose and Eastman had suggested we change the name of the group from *The Tonix* to *Sylvia Leon and the Tonix*. I could see the writing on the wall. With the first bit of success it would be 'Bye-bye band and hello Sylvia Leon, solo artiste.' I had seen it all before and was not going to be a part of it. The rest of the group, back in Harrogate, all had jobs, so the idea was that Sylvia would use me and Simon, with the rest of the musicians to be found in London. I stayed the night at Irene and Mimi's flat and the following day we attended the meeting. It went exactly as I imagined. It was agreed that the name would be changed to *Sylvia Leon and The Tonix*. We would all sign a new agreement and record a single with Sylvia. Sylvia needed us both present as we knew all her material. We recorded the single with some session musicians and returned to Harrogate, only to learn, predictably, that the drummer had finished with the group. This was the nail in the coffin for me. I began thinking of what to do next. I did not have to think long.

— CHAPTER ELEVEN —

The Great Train Robbery

John, who I shared the flat with in Harrogate, told me he had received a telephone call from his mate, the one who played lead guitar with Marty Wilde. They were looking for a rhythm guitarist for the following Saturday. Marty was playing at Ware in Hertfordshire. John had said that he would do it, and told his friend that he knew all of Marty's songs. The group were unsure but agreed to try him out if he arrived at the venue early for a quick rehearsal. He asked me if I would like to accompany him. I had already told John what was happening in *The Tonix*, perhaps this might be a way of finding alternative work. But first I had to tell the band I was leaving. They were not very pleased, to say the least. But I knew what would happen when we got to London: Sylvia would be getting more and more work on her own, the group would be faded into the background, and eventually they would not be needed anymore. Which is exactly what happened. Sylvia went on to become a successful solo recording artiste, and did many television shows in the '60s.

On Saturday morning I left with John, though not before trying to teach him how to bar the chords. He still couldn't get it, but the show that night at Ware was excellent. John nervously managed to survive the evening and I had my chat with Marty in the dressing room afterwards. He gave me his phone number and told me to call him. That evening, John was staying in a place near Edgware Road belonging to some of his friends, while I was to stay with Mimi and Irene. I left my equipment in his van, as I didn't want to make a noise carrying it downstairs in the early hours of the morning. John had Mimi's address and phone number and said he would drop it off to me the next day. The next morning he rang me with some bad news. The van had been broken into and my Fender bass guitar had been stolen, though they had left my amplifier and speakers. I thought that was very strange. John arrived and was very apologetic. Now I had no job and no bass and I was in a worse situation than had ever been. I did have a guitar back at my parent's home in Wales. Maybe I could part exchange it for a second-hand bass guitar? John drove me down and we stayed two nights. I spent one of the two days with Roy and Ken catching up on all the news. They had now formed a new outfit and were about to start working the clubs again.

When we arrived back in London, I exchanged my guitar for an old Hofner bass and immediately rang Marty Wilde. Marty invited me to his home in Blackheath for an audition. I found him to be a very kind and considerate man. He handed me a bass guitar and told me he was going to play a record and wanted me to play along with it. The record he put on was 'Lucille' by Little Richard. As it was one of my favourite records, I found it easy playing bass to it. I played along with a couple more records and Marty seemed satisfied. We had a coffee and he explained that he had some recordings planned and would be in touch in the not-too-distant future. Fate had decided that I was now back in London. I was staying once again with Irene and Mimi.

A few days later Marty rang and asked me to meet him at the *Regent Sound Recording Studios* in Denmark Street. Denmark Street was home to the *La Gioconda Café* (known as *The Gio*), a place I would frequent many times in the future. In fact it would become like a second home to me.

At the studio, Marty handed me the bass. It was a five-string model, which I had not encountered before. He asked me to play the bass run on a song called 'Jezebel'. Afterwards he wanted to re-record his 1958 hit 'Endless Sleep', adding the sound of seagulls in the background, inspired, I think, by the *Shangri-Las'* hit 'Walking in the Sand'. Marty was a very good musician and, I have to admit, I struggled for a bit. But I finally got the hang of the five string bass, with that added low B string, and began to hold my own. In my break, I visited the *Gioconda* café and ate some bread pudding, which cost four old pence, and then it was over to *The George* pub on Charing Cross Road for a quick pint. On my way back I bumped into Tommy Woodward – that's how I still thought of him; I'm not sure if by then he had taken our advice and changed his name to Tom Jones. He was wandering over to the *Gioconda*. I was surprised to see he was on his own. I asked how he was getting on. He seemed a bit fed up and said that Gordon was off somewhere trying to get a deal for him. I told him I hoped everything would go well but I had to get back to Regent Sound. He asked me if I was recording there. I explained about Marty and asked Tom if he would like to meet him. Perhaps he might be able to put something Tom's way.

'Yeah, great,' was the reply, so I took him to the studio and introduced him to Marty. The three of us chatted together for a while, with me telling Marty what a great voice Tommy had. Marty, being his usual self, said that if he could help Tom in any way, he would. But it was a short conversation because we had work to get on with. We said our goodbyes and carried on with the recording session.

Marty and I recorded a few songs that session, but the one he wanted to release was called 'No Love Have I/Ivory Tower'. He arranged a photo shoot and was negotiating with, I believe, Island Records. At the last minute, however, he informed me that he had fallen out with someone at the record company, and would be trying to get a release on it elsewhere. I believe at the time he was thinking of forming a trio and going into cabaret with his wife, Joyce, and another musician. Joyce had previously been a member of *The Vernons Girls*. I believe he had me in mind for the job, but I wasn't interested in playing the cabaret circuit. So that was that. In February 1965 Marty advertised in *Melody Maker* for a guitarist to work with him and his wife, and 'Ivory Tower' was forgotten. Justin Hayward answered the add, and he, Marty and Joyce became *The Wilde Three*, releasing a record entitled 'Since You've Gone' in April 1965 on the Decca label. Justin went on to become the guitarist and lead singer of *The Moody Blues*.

Meanwhile, Mimi and I had started a relationship. Well, it was more of a casual affair at the time and I didn't know if it was going anywhere. In the flat above us lived a slightly older couple. I shall call them Arthur and Sheryl. We were friendly with both of them, but mainly with Sheryl. Arthur was more of a recluse, and on the rare occasions he did appear, was never seen without dark glasses and a generally shifty air. We were told Arthur was a big time bookie, but I had my doubts: what would a big time bookie be doing renting a flat in Tolmer Square? Today Tolmer Square is a very sought-after location, being so near to the West End, but in those days, needless to say, things were a little different! Of course, it was perfect for us musicians. At the time we didn't realise that Eric Clapton was living with his girlfriend on the top floor. We only found out when Arthur threw him down the stairs for making a noise; it was always quiet after that.

Sheryl visited Mimi's flat quite regularly and we had many a long chat with her. Arthur, on the other hand, was a different kettle of fish. The only time I would ever see him was if we crossed paths in the corridor. He would brush past me, always in a hurry, and the most I would ever get out of him was a 'Mmm' or a grunt – shifty wasn't the word for him.

One afternoon I returned to find the square surrounded by police. Apparently they were searching Arthur and Sheryl's flat. We had heard rumours that Arthur's parents ran a pub in the East End and that one day a couple had come in and asked them if they could leave a bag behind the bar for safekeeping; that this bag was somehow connected to the Great Train Robbery. I still don't really know if any of this was true or not.

But what I did hear on the grapevine is that the police raided the pub and some of the money from the Great Train Robbery was found in the bag. I was told the police were going to charge Arthur's parents for having stolen money on the premises.

It is said that there were two further people connected to the Great Train Robbery who were never caught. Was one of them Arthur? Who knows? What I do know, from friends at the time, was that Arthur and Sheryl, after moving out of Tolmer Square, bought a Rolls Royce and ended up living in a Mews Cottage near the centre of London.

By frequenting the *Gioconda* café in Denmark Street more regularly, I began meeting and becoming friendly with people who worked in the recording and publishing business, and, of course, I began hanging out with many more musicians, some who were in the same predicament as myself. Downstairs from the *Gioconda* was *Central Sound Recording Studio* owned by Freddy Winrose. The main entrance to the studio was next to that for the *Gioconda*, but it also had a side entrance inside the café, halfway between the front door and the counter. In those days, it was just a small four-track studio, but Freddy made it work – he had a sound maybe to rival Joe Meek's. A number of early hit records came out of the studio before being passed on to the major companies, including early *Rolling Stones* recordings. If he were ever in the middle of a recording session and needed an extra musician, Freddy would come up into the *Gioconda* and ask around. I would sit there hour after hour waiting for some recording work, as did many other musicians. Some days I would have to put my bread pudding on tick and settle up when I had earned some money from a recording session later that day. Other times it might be a week or two before I could settle the bill. The owner always trusted us to pay up, and usually everybody did. After all, it was in our interest to pay: the *Gioconda* acted as the main meeting place for musicians; it was our office and contact location for recording work. Over the years, I did quite a few sessions for Freddy and played on many records. The money wasn't brilliant, but at least I was earning something. I believe that the *Gioconda* is still there, but the current owners have changed the spelling of the name to *Giaconda*.

It was still 1964, yet so many things had happened in just a few months it seemed like a lifetime had passed. *The Ship* pub in Wardour Street, together with *The George* in Charing Cross Road, was the main hangout for musicians. I would also be invited to the *147 Club*, just around the corner from Denmark Street. That too would become important to me, but for now, I was a jobbing bass player, filling in with bands and doing a few recording sessions. In my spare time, to earn some extra money, I had a job in a little club in Gerrard Street. In those days Gerard Street was full of small clubs, including *Ronnie Scott's Jazz Club*. Now it is part of Chinatown. My job, with one of the heavies on hand, was to take the money at the door, making sure everyone paid. If someone left the club, they had to pay again to get back in, even if they had previously paid. It was a great little club, and I quite liked working there. I became friendly with all sorts of people: musicians, actors, villains and prostitutes. It was a busy club and I worked all through the night until five or six the following morning, in the process becoming friendly with a regular, a Welsh lad who they called Taffy. They called most people from Wales Taffy in those days. He was from Tredegar and was a nice guy, but he had a drug problem. The main drug in those days was Purple Hearts, the street name for Dexamyl (or Drinamil), a habit-forming stimulant which was rife around the London clubs. Taffy unfortunately was mixing them with alcohol. I tried many times to persuade him to stop taking the drugs, but to no avail. He was a character and well-known to most people in the music business, but he was losing weight rapidly. In the end, through his behaviour, they had to ban him from the club, and a few weeks later, I heard he had died from alcohol and drug abuse.

— CHAPTER TWELVE —

My Worst Ever Gig

1964 passed, and by April 1965, we were living in Beaumont Mews and Mimi was pregnant. Beaumont Mews had an entrance off Marylebone High Street, and a second entrance off Weymouth Street. It was London W1, near Harley Street, and one of the most sought-after addresses in the whole city. Cliff Richard lived about fifty yards away, in a flat over the Pricerite supermarket on Marylebone High Street. But I've got to say, at first, I didn't want to take it. It was expensive. Working at the club and doing some recording sessions was bringing in some money, but couldn't really be relied upon. Irene still had her own flat, but for the time being she was helping us out with the rent. Inside it was actually quite small – upstairs we had small lounge, one bedroom, a small bathroom and a tiny kitchen. Underneath was a garage, but we did not have access to that.

Irene had negotiated a deal for us with the owner of the property, who she had met at one of the hotels where she worked. Irene worked nights on the switchboard at these hotels and, in those days, the switchboards were located near the lobby, so she could see everyone coming and going. If a big star had booked in and they were taking someone up to their room late at night, she would turn a blind eye, and they appreciated that, and trusted her not to give information to the press. She became known to many a famous name over the years and was rewarded handsomely by some. Years before I met her, the famous film comedy duo Bud Abbott and Lou Costello had taken Irene and Mimi out shopping in a hired Rolls Royce whilst on a break from filming.

Our only problem was that if anyone famous stayed at the hotel she would try to tell them about her showbiz daughter Mimi – and now about me as well. We would get occasional telephone calls from Irene, usually late at night, saying, 'I've just been speaking to so and so they're really nice. Hang on, they want to speak to you.' She would then put us through to some celebrity or other at the other end of the line, and we would have no idea what to say to them. She even put Brian Epstein through one evening. It completely threw me off guard; all I could say was that I had played *The Cavern* and that I knew Bob Wooler. Irene came back on the line and said he would like to speak to Mimi. She had told Brian that Mimi had been a dancer but now she was a singer and was going to be a big star – she hadn't sung a note in her life. Mimi spluttered something down the phone, panicked, and put the receiver down. That's what Irene was like: always trying to get Mimi into the business. Years previously, if Mimi had an audition to attend, Irene would run ahead and tell the person in charge that her daughter was on her way. Mimi was probably still at home putting her make up on.

Shortly after speaking to Brian Epstein, Mimi decided that she did actually want to be a singer, and so we started rehearsals together. It was hard work; she had never sung before and couldn't sing harmonies, so it was left to her to sing the lead vocal. After many weeks of rehearsal, when we thought our vocals were good enough, we did an audition for an agency that was based near us in Blandford Street. The agent said he thought we were very good, but not quite ready for the big time, and advised us to go back and continue rehearsing, which we did. After more weeks of unrelenting rehearsals we made a return trip to the agent; this time he liked us and promised to procure us some work. A few weeks went by and then, unexpectedly, we received a telephone call from the agent, asking us if we would like to do a late spot in the West End. We jumped at the chance; the venue was to be *The Freddie Mills Night Club* in Charing Cross Road. Freddie Mills had become world light heavyweight champion in 1948 and later had ventured into the world of show business, appearing in two *Carry On* films, television variety shows, pop shows, children's television, as well as writing a weekly boxing column for a Sunday newspaper. He also opened a restaurant, which he later decided to convert into a nightclub.

We were on at midnight, and Mimi had invited some friends along. We were introduced to Freddie, who, I may say, was an extremely likable person and very kind to us. We were due to play an acoustic set with just the one guitar. There was one microphone set up in the middle of the floor for the vocals and another set up for my guitar. There would be nowhere to hide, either sonically or visually, and I could tell Mimi was daunted. The club was well-known, and Freddie had told us there would be a few showbiz personalities in that evening, which made her even more nervous. At five minutes to midnight, we were standing at the entrance to the cabaret floor waiting for the compère to introduce us. Even for me, this was a long way from the workingmen's clubs of south Wales, the *2i's* Coffee Bar and the smoke-filled rock and blues clubs of London. For Mimi, it must have been a hundred times more intimidating. By now, she had become so nervous that unbeknown to me she began twiddling with the tuning pegs on my guitar. I had already tuned the guitar up ready for our appearance and didn't have a clue what she was doing. I was too busy looking out into the club eyeing up the audience, trying to see what stars were in. Then, on the stroke of midnight, we were on. I strummed the first chord and it was so out of tune, I could not believe it. Mimi had started to sing, so I started the harmony whilst still trying to tune the guitar, but I couldn't concentrate on both. In hindsight, I should have stopped and re-tuned the guitar whilst I did a bit of chat with the audience.

However, I had never done a cabaret spot before. I had only played rock and blues clubs. So we ploughed on with the song. But Mimi was so off key that it led to my harmonies being off as well. Moreover, the guitar, by now, was more out of tune than ever. I could hear people's laughter in the background. They must have thought we were a comedy act. We kept going until the end of the song, but when we finished there was no applause, just a few snickers of laughter. Through the glare of the spotlight I could see the laughter on some of the faces, while others had that cringing look, the look I had seen many times before when I had been starting out in the social clubs. I said, 'Thank you,' then turned to Mimi and whispered, 'Say something while I tune up.'

She leaned towards the microphone and said... 'Thank you.' That was it!

I told her to keep talking so she introduced the next song, which took all of six or seven seconds. I whispered, 'Say something else, keep talking!'

She came back with, 'It's a lovely song.'

All the while I was trying to tune the guitar, which seemed so loud with the club being so quiet, but by now I was panicking, and the more I tuned the worse it got. I tried to make light of it, saying, 'I paid five pounds for this guitar five years ago, and it's gone out of tune.'

A voice shouted out, 'Take it back then, you can't play it.'

I ignored this. 'Anyone know any jokes?'

Back came the reply: 'Yes, you!'

I eventually managed to get it roughly in tune. We did a few more numbers that sounded somewhat better, got a bit of applause, and said goodnight. It had been Mimi's first ever professional singing gig, and looking back, it would have been wise for us to have turned the booking down and started somewhere other than a top nightclub, somewhere smaller, like a pub. Just as we were preparing our exit, Freddie sent for us. He was sitting on his own, at a table situated at the side of the cabaret floor. I thought he was going to really have a go at us, but the first thing he said was, 'Mm, Roger and Mimi, that's an unusual name.' Then he ordered us drinks and we sat talking for some time. What a night!

A few weeks later Freddie was dead, shot through the eye whilst sitting in his car at the rear of the club. Some say he committed suicide because he was in debt. A week or two previously he had borrowed a rifle from a friend who owned a shooting gallery. Although the rifle was not in working order when borrowed, it had been repaired and was found in the car alongside him. At the time, gangsters were extorting money from London club owners and they say Freddie was in debt to them. Another theory was that London's Chinatown was relocating from Limehouse in East London to Soho, and that some shady characters wanted Freddie's club to be turned into a Chinese restaurant. Third was that Freddie was secretly a homosexual (the term 'gay' was not used in those days) and that he killed himself rather than let it become public knowledge. Homosexuality was not decriminalised in the UK until 1967. Then there was the theory that Freddie was the unidentified serial killer known as Jack the Stripper, who had between 1959 and 1965 murdered at least eight prostitutes, removed their clothes (hence the name Jack the Stripper) and dumped their bodies around the river Thames. One leading London crime figure, who was writing a book on the subject, said he had evidence to prove Freddie was the killer, but his work was never published. Years later one of the Sunday papers wrote an article stating that Freddie had had an affair with the late singer Michael Holliday. Michael reached number one in the charts twice, with 'The Story of My Life' in 1958 and 'Starry Eyed' in 1959. They also stated that rumours were circulating that Freddie had also had an affair with Ronnie Kray, one of the Kray twins. The openly bisexual Ronnie Kray fiercely denied this. All speculation?

It was the middle of August 1965 – two months away from

the birth of Mimi's and my first child. I decided to head for the *The Ship* and find some work. I got into conversation with a musician named Noel, who I had previously met in 1964. Noel was a guitarist and also played bass. He was leaving to go to *The 147 Club* in Charing Cross Road and said I could accompany him if I wanted. *The 147 Club* was situated more or less opposite *The Freddie Mills Night Club*. It was located on the first floor, small, with a small bar and a roulette table. If you fancied a bet, you could use coins on the table instead of chips. It was early evening, and the crowd was thin on the ground. Noel introduced me to the barmaid, whose name was Theresa. I bought a drink and Noel led me to the other side of the room, over to a table where a man was sitting alone. He introduced me to Brian Poole. Brian was lead singer with the band *Brian Poole and The Tremolos*. He had had a number four in the charts with 'Twist and Shout' and a number one with 'Do You Love Me' on Decca Records. Dick Rowe, who was the label boss at Decca at the time, in 1962 had had a choice to sign either *The Beatles* or *Brian Poole and The Tremeloes* (then just called *The Tremeloes*). He chose Brian and the band because he thought they were more commercial and because they were based locally. When *The Beatles* finally became famous, Dick became known as the man who turned them down. I had a good long conversation with Brian; his advice to me was never give up, and that perseverance was worth fifty per cent of talent. I still believe that today.

A few weeks later, I started rehearsals with Noel in a cellar in Soho. Noel was playing lead guitar with a group that was being put together solely as a backing outfit, and I was roped in to play bass. The group didn't have a name, and there was no mention of recordings or work, but apparently a guitarist/singer would be coming over from America to be our frontman. Johnny Winter was his name. I had never heard of him and, in a way, I was glad when he decided to cancel his trip. I had got fed up rehearsing for something that might never happen. I was still working nights at the club in Gerard Street, as well as doing some recording work in the afternoons. It was all getting too much for me. I went back to *The 147 Club* and tried to amass as many contacts as I could. Noel stayed with the band until 1966 when he went for an audition he thought was for the lead guitar spot in *The Animals*. But Chas Chandler, the former bassists for *The Animals* and the man who I believe was originally behind the plan to bring over Johnny Winter, had pulled the wool over Noel's eyes. The audition wasn't for *The Animals*, but to back up another American guitarist who was on his way over to London. You may have heard of him: Jimi Hendrix. Chas asked Noel if he could play bass. He did, and he was in – the rest is history. Noel Redding became part of *The Jimi Hendrix Experience* and went onto fame and glory.

One night, on a visit to inspect his business, the owner of the club introduced me to the singer Paul Korda. He was unknown then, but in years to come his songs would be recorded by Roger Daltrey, Frankie Valli and Dave Edmunds.

Paul told me he had written a song entitled 'Eyes' and was looking for some finance to record it. The club owner overheard our conversation and said if it was any good, he would back it. Paul managed to procure a guitar from somewhere, played the song, and that was it: the owner was hooked. But if it were to be recorded, it would need a B-side. Paul asked me if I had any ideas. I had always liked the song 'Unchained Melody'. It had been a hit in the USA years earlier for Al Hibbler and later again in Britain for Jimmy Young. Paul asked if I would like to sing it with him, so in the following days we worked out the harmonies. We recorded both numbers, and the club owner loved 'Unchained Melody'. He said that it was the best version he had ever heard. But then Paul went off to try to get a deal with one of the record companies, and that was the last we saw of him. I was on my own once more.

My son Cary was born at the Middlesex Hospital in October 1965 and, at the time, we were still living at Beaumont Mews. He was born with light ginger colour hair which later turned jet black. He was a very happy little soul, not one to burst out crying every few minutes. We were now finding it even more difficult to manage the rent. I was filling in as a bass player for a variety of groups and, by this time, was singing lead vocal too. Some nights after finishing a booking, I would end up working at the club in Gerard Street, whilst a few afternoons a week were spent in the *Gioconda* waiting for some recording sessions. Theresa, the barmaid at *The 147 Club*, introduced me to Tony Marsh, who was the compère on many of the pop package tours of the time. In those days a compère was needed to introduce the bands on stage; after all, who had ever heard of Donovan? There would also be a comedian on these tours, and one of them, a certain Des O'Connor, would ultimately take over compère duties from Tony. Through Tony, I was introduced to many of the great and good of the London music scene, and though I didn't stay in touch with a lot of them, my friendship with both him and Theresa continued for many years.

Dave the drummer, who had driven Roy and Ken home and told me he would be back in London the following day, had turned up almost a year later. Apparently, on his return home, Dave had met a local girl, and that was the reason for his delay. Dave and his girlfriend, Margaret, had travelled back to London and rented a flat over in Hackney, where Margaret had managed to find work in a local factory. They would visit us almost every Sunday. Margaret would constantly complain about Dave, saying that she worked herself to the bone whilst Dave did nothing. He would have butter on his toast and sandwiches, whilst she would only be allowed margarine. She wasn't allowed a full cigarette; he would smoke three quarters of it and leave her the last quarter – or the nip end, as we used to call it. This went on Sunday after Sunday until, in the end, we got wise and made sure we were out on that day. I believe that Dave did eventually get work as a drummer, with a London-based Welsh band, before returning home to team up again with Roy and Ken who, once again, had become very successful on the Welsh circuit.

When we thought all that was over, Dave Coombs, the vicar's son who had managed Dave and me in *The Z Men*, turned up on our doorstep. He had also travelled to London to try to get work. He wasn't with us when we worked Liverpool or when we lived in London at Westbourne Park Road; he had only wanted to manage us locally in Wales. Now he was here, his girlfriend in tow, asking me for a loan of twenty pounds for a deposit on a flat. That would be roughly two hundred and twenty pounds at today's rate. We were nearly skint ourselves. He didn't like it when I told him I didn't have the money; he probably thought we were rolling in it because of where we lived. He stormed off in a huff, never to be seen again.

By April 1966, our money situation had worsened. We were behind with the rent and we were now being hassled by the property owner, so we decided to do a moonlight flit. We found a room in a house in Ladbroke Grove, near the corner with Elgin Crescent. It was on the first floor of a three storey building with a further basement flat underneath. Going from the luxury of Beaumont Mews to the downmarket area of Ladbroke Grove was a bit of a downgrade. In fact, in comparison, even the flat I had rented with the band in Westbourne Park Road was pure luxury. The room, which smelled of damp, had a double bed and a washbasin, a coin-slot gas meter situated underneath the washbasin, and that was it. We put most of our furniture into storage, and the belongings we did bring with us were piled into one corner of the room, almost reaching ceiling height. But if we thought that was bad, there was a whole lot worse to come. We had problems as soon as we moved in. The couple underneath accused us of spying on them through the floorboards! There were so many boxes and other stuff piled up around the room it would have been near impossible to pull the carpet up and make holes in the floor to spy on someone. And what did we want to spy on them for anyway? But these accusations went on for a couple of days until, one afternoon, I heard heavy footsteps coming up the stairs – the man's, I guessed – then a loud knocking on our door. I'd had enough! I swung the door open, ready to confront him. But just as I opened my mouth to give him a piece of my mind, his eyes darted down to my acoustic guitar, which was standing up against a box near the doorway.

'Is that a Levin?' he asked.

I was taken aback 'Yes, What about it?'

The Levin guitar I owned was made in Sweden. It was an excellent guitar, a model very much sought after today. The man asked if he could have a play. I could not believe this was the same guy who for the past few days had been accusing us of spying: he was all smiles now. I let him try it out – anything to keep the peace – and he told me his name was Davey Graham. He said he was a folk-cum-blues singer/songwriter and was playing the folk clubs in the West End. He said he'd had trouble with the previous tenants, but he could now see that our floor was covered in boxes. He apologised, and told me that his partner had been paranoid about the previous tenants living in our room, and that someone had told her that we were friends of theirs.

Both being musicians, we became very friendly, and he invited me to watch him play at Les Cousins, a folk club in Soho. I was shocked to say the least. This guy was great, his guitar playing was superb, and he had such a huge following. I couldn't believe that someone with his talent was living in a dump in Ladbroke Grove. In the sixties, Davey popularised the DADGAD tuning for the guitar; it's a special tuning still used today by many folk guitarists, and he went on to inspire so many legends of music, such as Paul Simon, Jimmy Page, Richie Blackmore, Ray Davies, and many more top guitarists. His composition 'Angi' is featured on Simon and Garfunkel's worldwide hit album *The Sound of Silence*, though there it is renamed 'Anji'. We remained friends until Davey and his partner moved on, I believe after receiving some recording royalties. We then moved to his room on the ground floor. It was much the same as ours, but it was a lot easier than negotiating a steep staircase with a pram down to the ground floor.

— CHAPTER THIRTEEN —
Hiding from the Police

We needed money fast, so I found a local job through a friend who was working as part of a maintenance team in Notting Hill. I did all manner of jobs: from cleaning to painting, whatever needed doing, we did it. There were three of us: Shaun, an out of work actor; a young American guy named Toby, who was travelling the world; and me. The money wasn't too bad, and it was a good laugh. I got to know a few of the residents, one of whom was the actor Andrew Ray, the son of the late comedian Ted Ray. Madeline Bell was a frequent visitor. She was then a backing singer for Dusty Springfield and later went on to join Blue Mink and have six top twenty singles.

It was around this time, one evening, that Cary had a convulsion. Neither of us knew what was happening and I thought he was dying. I picked him up and ran out of the building with Mimi trailing behind me. We were both now running up Ladbroke grove. A black cab eventually stopped and we headed for the nearest hospital. We were eventually told that he had a really high temperature. They kept him in hospital and his temperature eventually subsided. What a relief, it had been a really frightening experience.

Although I was missing the music scene, I was happy working at Hedgegate Court. Not that, really, I had a choice in the matter: I could not do both my job and my music, and we needed the money, so this job came first. Mimi wasn't working; her leg had virtually healed, but she now had Cary to look after. Irene helped when she could, but with two jobs she could only do so much. Money was tight, to say the least, but we were surviving. But then our landlord and his wife, a Vietnamese couple who lived in the basement flat, decided to put all the tenants' rents up by a pound a week. This might not seem a lot of money today but in 1966 it was equivalent of around eleven or twelve pounds. There was just no way we could afford it.

The electric meter took one shilling and two shilling coins, and the landlord would empty it on a weekly basis. At some point he must have altered the timing on the meter as the amount of electricity that was supplied for a shilling suddenly seemed to have been cut by half. So a friend, who was an expert at fiddling the electric meters, took the old lead seal off, then clocked the meter somehow, so that we would have practically double the amount of electricity. He then replaced the old seal with an identical new one. It was a joy to see the landlord's face every week as he emptied the meter. He couldn't understand why there was so little money in it. I would always say that we couldn't afford to have the fire on or cook. 'Can't you see we're getting thinner?' I would ask.

But it wasn't enough, and once more, we were getting into debt. After a few weeks the landlord began banging on our door. We locked it from the inside and waited him out. Friends suggested that we contact the rent tribunal because of the extortionate rent he was now charging; once we informed the tribunal there would be nothing legally he could do until the case was heard. In those days, there were so many unscrupulous property owners in London that the government had set up the rent tribunal for tenants to voice their concerns. The tribunal would, if necessary, adjust the rent if they thought it was unfair.

We did this, and when our day came round, we won our case. The rent was to be lowered; the only problem was we had to pay back some of the arrears. I told the tribunal we could not afford to pay it back even on a weekly basis. Because of this, the tribunal gave us a month to leave the premises. In the days that followed, we had so much hassle from the landlord and his wife. They threatened us, saying that they were going to get some of their people to shift us out. If they only knew the contacts we had around the West End... But we said nothing and just continued looking for another place to live.

It all came to a head one evening when Irene came to visit us. As she was walking up the steps to the front door the landlord and landlady came out of their basement flat and started shouting abuse at her, telling her that we shouldn't be living there as were not paying any rent and that she was as bad as us. I heard the commotion and rushed out to see what was happening. By the time I got there, Irene was really riled up and having a go right back at them. I tried to calm things down, but the landlord came at me in a rage, throwing a punch that missed me. In those days, growing up in the coal mining valleys of south Wales in the '40s and '50s, you had to learn how to defend yourself or you'd never survive. I grabbed his arm and tried to pull him over, but he was too heavy; back he came at me again. I rolled onto the floor and kicked his legs from under him and he went down. The only trouble was he didn't stay down, and as he was getting up Irene laid into him, hitting him over the head with her bag; he lost his balance and went down again. We learned later that while he and Irene had been arguing, his wife had called the police; she wanted them to believe that we were causing all the trouble. So just as he was picking himself up again the police arrived, saw Irene laying into him with her bag, took his word that I had started it, arrested me, and took me to Notting Hill Police Station, where I spent the night!

The next evening I was released without charge. The police had checked out the facts I had given them about the rent tribunal and how the landlord was illegally trying to get us out. They had also checked with the neighbours and they had told them that he was harassing us. They had a word with him and from then on, until the time we moved, we had no further problems with him.

We managed to find a third floor flat in Balcombe Street, Marylebone, NW1. The street would become international news in 1975 when four IRA gunmen held a couple hostage for six days – it became known as The Balcombe Street Siege. The flat was located on the top floor and to say it wasn't up to much would be an understatement; we both decided that we wouldn't stay long. Every flat below us was empty and the front door had to be left on the latch: anyone could walk into the building. We had a key for our own flat but not for the front door. It was dark and eerie inside the hallway, which was lit only by a single bulb. The walls were brown and dirty with bits peeling off, and there seemed to be dust everywhere. Skirting boards were missing in the hallway, there were holes in the walls and bits of plaster had fallen from the ceiling. The stairs were bare, old and creaking, and again lit only by a single bulb, located on the first floor, the light of which grew dimmer and dimmer as you progressed further up to the top floor. With no other tenants in the building, coupled with the peeling walls, creaking floors, and the dim lighting it looked like something out of a horror film. On the way upstairs some of the doors to the empty flats would be wide open. I looked inside one once; it was the same as the hallway, full of dust and rubble. We were told before moving in that someone had been living in the top flat, the one we were renting, but had recently moved out. I wonder why?

Years earlier, when we had first come to London with the band, Dave the drummer and I wanted to upgrade our equipment. Dave really wanted the latest set of Premier drums and I had my eye a big new bass cabinet that had just come out. They were expensive items, but Irene said she would sign a guarantee for them. I don't know what name she gave. We thought we were on a roll and it would be no bother paying it back, but we were wrong.

When Dave fancied a trip back to Wales, he would offer me a lift. On one of these trips we had to call into Blackwood police station. I think Dave had been stopped and had to produce his driving documents. It was all very straightforward, we thought nothing of it, and afterwards Dave dropped me at my parents' house. But someone at the police station must have checked on his name, because a few hours later a police van arrived at my parents' home. They hauled me out of the house and into the back of the van. Dave was already sat in there, waiting for me. We were taken to Blackwood Police Station, where we spent the night. The following day two plain clothed police officers arrived from London, handcuffed us and took us back to Paddington Police Station by train. There had been an arrest warrant out for the both of us. I can't imagine today that they would send two police officers from London to escort someone back to Paddington Police Station for a hire purchase debt. A day later we were in court. Fortunately we were let off a fine, as long as we agreed to pay up what was owing on the debt, which we eventually did.

I'd had enough of police for a while, but my apparent criminal career was only just beginning. One evening in the Balcombe Street flat at around 11.00pm, two uniformed police officers arrived at the flat door. The door to the street, as I said previously, was always on the latch; we couldn't lock it. I was down the corridor at the time. I think bagging up the rubbish. I heard one of the police officers tell Mimi that they had an arrest warrant for me. Apparently I had stolen a car. After the relatively recent ordeal with the police, I couldn't handle another night in a cell, so I crept down to the empty flat below. Just as I did so, I heard the police say that they were going to search the premises. I hid in the cupboard under the sink, rolled myself up and waited. The clomping of their boots came through the ceiling, then after about ten or twelve minutes I heard one of them say, 'When you see him tell him to get in touch. Otherwise it'll only get worse for him.'

Then I could hear them coming downstairs. My heart was racing, the back of my head was forced against the top of the cupboard, my knees dug into face, and my body ached. I was hoping they would go straight out, but no, I could hear them trying the door of the flat opposite. Then the sound of their boots on the bare floorboards as they searched the flat. After a short while they were out. Their footsteps came closer. I heard them try the door of the flat that I was in. Why hadn't I put something behind the door? Maybe the lock was working on the inside; I could have put the snib up. But it was too late! They were in.

A voice blurted out, 'You in here, Simmonds?' I thought about Ken, he would have probably answered, 'Yes, what do you fucking want?'

The sound of their boots got louder. I could see the occasional flash from their torches through the small cracks in the cupboard. I could hear them clomping from room to room, and now they were coming into the kitchen.

'He's not here,' one of them said, but as he did so he slid open the door to the cupboard under the sink – the same cupboard I was in, only further along. My heart was beating like the clappers. I felt sure they would hear it. I was sweating and my breathing was heavy. If they opened the other door to the cupboard, it was all over. But then the cupboard was slid closed again, and the sound of their boots began to recede. I remained in the cupboard for some time, listening to their boots echoing around the building as they made their way down to the ground floor, searching every flat as they went. At one point, one police officer told the other what a dump the place was, and remarked that whatever I had done, we shouldn't be living in a place like this.

Eventually I heard them leave. I waited at least a half an hour just in case they doubled back and then I returned to our flat upstairs. Mimi wanted to know where the hell I had got to.

When the police turned up at my parents' home and told them that there was a warrant out for my arrest, they assumed that it was for the hire purchase debt. The guy who told the police that I had stolen his car had lived in the same village as my parents but had now moved out. My friends at home had no idea where he had gone. I knew the police wanted to question me about the incident, but I had no idea there was an arrest warrant out for me. My 'offence' had supposedly occurred around eighteen months previously on a trip back to Wales.

I had been home to visit my parents and I was in a local pub. Some friends that I hadn't seen for years walked in. They were not involved in the music industry, just pals I had gone to school with. They were off to Cardiff for the night and asked if I'd like join them. I readily agreed. I had not been to Cardiff for a few years and thought it would be great to pay the *New Moon Club* a visit again. So, after we finished our drinks, we were off. Lawrence, one of the boys, had been my best friend at school, and we spent the entire journey catching up. Colin, the person driving the car, had just moved to Wales with his parents from the West Country. Lawrence and Keith, my two friends, had not known him long. He didn't say much and I'm not exactly sure what it was, but I didn't take to him at all.

After listening to a great band in one of the Cardiff clubs we bypassed *The New Moon Club* and had a pint in *The Custom House* pub, slowly making our way down to the Bay area. In those days it was called Tiger Bay; you might recognise it from the lyrics of Ian Dury's 1978 hit 'Hit Me with Your Rhythm Stick'. Bute Street, the main thoroughfare to the Bay, was a notorious area for prostitutes. We used to call it The Bute. Colin had been drinking the same amount as us (there were no breathalyser tests at that time; they didn't come into use in the UK until 1967), but as he sped the car erratically down the street, I was getting worried. It still wasn't that late and we had plenty of drinking time to go. I said to Lawrence that I didn't think we would get back if he drank anymore. Lawrence had a full licence, Keith couldn't drive and I only had a provisional license. If push came to shove Lawrence said that he would drive home.

The Bay in those days was a very rough area. There were nationalities from every corner of the globe, mostly merchant seamen. From *The Custom House* we headed on down to *The Ship and Pilot*; neither pub has survived to the present day, but they tell me that there is a new *Ship and Pilot* down there now. In *The Ship and Pilot* I remember having a laugh with the landlord; he had previously been involved in the entertainment business and I was telling him about the time our group had played at *The New Moon Club*. He said that he knew the owner's son, Peter, and then proceeded to tell me that Shirley Bassey had sang a few times at *The Ship and Pilot*. That's when Colin came out with, 'No wonder she moved!'

Keith pulled him to the side and threatened that if he ever said anything like that again, he'd lay him out. He was right; we were in the wrong area to take the piss. After *The Ship and Pilot*, we headed for a late drink and some food. We found ourselves entering a small rough-looking bar. As we went up to order something to eat, Colin bent over, looked into plate of food a woman was eating, his nose about four inches from the plate and said, 'Looks fucking awful,' then rising up commented, 'and she don't look much better.'

The woman had a sharp knife in her hand similar to a steak knife. She lashed out at him and he jumped backwards. It caught Lawrence on the wrist and blood started pouring everywhere. The woman did a runner, while the guy behind the bar tried wrapping a tea towel around the wound. Naturally the barman told us to get him to the infirmary quickly. Keith couldn't drive and Colin was pissed as a rat, so it was left to me.

We bundled him in the car and headed for the hospital. I knew where the hospital was. It wouldn't take that long. It would be no use calling for an ambulance down there in those days. God knows how long they would take. On the way we were stopped by the police for speeding, but once they saw the state of Lawrence, they escorted us to the hospital. Once Lawrence was safely inside, they started questioning me, taking my driving license number and insurance details. They then asked if it was it my car and, of course, I said no. I told the officer who the car belonged to and that he was in no condition to answer any questions. They asked Keith to pass Colin a message: to report to the police station the next day as they wanted to take a full statement. I gave my name and address, but because they couldn't interview Colin, they wanted me to accompany them to the police station. In the end they did relent and let us stay with Lawrence at the hospital.

I was booked for driving without a full license and no insurance. They said they could have booked me for having too much drink, but didn't because I drove really well. It was a small price to pay. My only concern was the injury to Lawrence. After stitching him up, they let us stay in the hospital that night, Lawrence on the recovery bed and us kipping down on the seats in the waiting area.

The following day, Lawrence, Keith and I caught the bus back to Nelson. We said our goodbyes and the next day I headed back to London a day late.

Apparently, when Colin was questioned at the police station they asked him if he had given me permission to drive the car and he answered no. The police then asked him if I had taken it without his permission and he answered yes. So they issued a warrant for me on the grounds that I took and drove away a vehicle without the consent of the owner, in effect stealing it. After the incident with the police in Balcombe Street, I got straight on to the Cardiff police. I told them exactly what happened. The owner had been in the car with me. Why then wasn't there also a warrant issued on a kidnapping charge? I said I would be straight down and they could arrest me and take me to court if they wanted, but they would look idiots as I had friends as witnesses. I also told them that I would be giving the story to the local newspapers. I did return, but in the meantime, they had been to interview Lawrence and Keith. The two officers in charge of the case, who it transpired had asked Colin leading questions, had their knuckle's rapped, and the case was eventually dropped.

I had told only two people in London about the incident, and those two knew that we were living in Balcombe Street. I had not even told my parents where we were living at the time because it was so bad. Those two so-called friends, for some reason, must have informed the police. In a way it was a good thing, because it was closure, and I had nothing more to hide. But still, the old saying had never seemed so true: *With friends like that, who needs enemies*.

The Bay wasn't all bad though. There was a singer in the '60s who hailed from there by the name of Gene Latter. Gene was born to Arabic parents and I believe came to London around 1965. I suppose in those days he would have been classed as a soul singer. I had met him briefly in Soho around 1966, just after the release, on Decca Records, of his cover of *The Rolling Stones* song 'Mother's little Helper'. Gene wrote and recorded some excellent material over the years but 'Mothers Little Helper' wasn't one of them. I remember him telling me at the time that *The Stones* hated his version. We lost touch for a few years, then I met him again in a club in 1967. He had just released the song 'A Little Piece of Leather', a classic number. We went out on the town to celebrate – both his hit and our reunion. I saw Gene around the West End on numerous occasions after that. He released records all through the '60s on many of the major labels, including the 1969 Northern Soul classic 'Sign on the Dotted Line', and in the same year 'Tiger Bay', named after the place where he was born. Gene was probably the only true soul singer to come out of Wales and should get recognition for that. Recently the DJ Brian Mathews played one of Gene's records on *Sounds of the Sixties*, his Saturday morning radio show, and after hearing it on Brian's programme, Chris Evans also played it on his morning Radio 2 show, saying what a great sound it was.

I last saw Gene in 1982, the evening before New Year's Eve. We met by chance in the West End. I was on my way to the station to head back to Wales, but Gene mentioned that a new club had opened recently near Marble Arch. He suggested we take a look. This we did, but on arrival found the club practically empty. We spent over an hour talking before I said my goodbyes and headed back to Wales to celebrate the New Year. My daughter Sasha is still very good friends with Gene's daughter, Yvonne, and his wife, Jean. Gene sadly passed away around 2005.

It was coming to the end of 1966 and we were desperate to leave Balcombe Street. Our minds were eventually made up for us when we discovered that the inside was going to be gutted. But with little money and a baby in tow, it wasn't going to be easy finding another place to live. Eventually, through one of Irene's contacts we took a room in Polygon Buildings, Phoenix Road, which was in the Somers town area of London. We took the room without viewing it. After Ladbroke Grove and Balcombe Street, how bad could it be?

My first night with *The Z Men* around 1962-63

The James Boys

One of Mimi's early publicity shots around 1964

Mimi publicity shot 1964

Me in Beaumont Mews 1965

Mimi posing in Beaumont Mews 1965

Decca publicity shot 1969

Decca handout 1969

Me, Maggie, Ray and John as *The New Honeycombs* 1971

Howard Lee, Keith Dangerfield, Me, Martin Murray 1971

Me and Maggie in 1972 – somewhere in the north East of England
We worked under the name of 'Cody and Candy'

Me and Maggie outside Ddraig Studios 1972

Me today 2016

— CHAPTER FOURTEEN —

Plunging to the Depths

When I first set eyes on Polygon Buildings my heart sank. It was a large old building that looked like a cross between an old Victorian workhouse and a prison. It even had its own prison yard at the front. Some of the windows in the building were smashed, and as I walked in, I could feel the ice-cold air blowing through on to my face.

Inside the building the walls were damp and peeling. Our room, situated on the ground floor, was tiny. It was just big enough for a single bed and a cot. There was no washbasin, toilet or water in the room, and no heating. We had brought some boxes with us. These were full of clothes, cooking utensils and other such items, but unfortunately we couldn't unpack them, as there was no space available in the room. The only floor space was the narrow pathway leading between the single bed and the cot. This was our lowest point! We had worked our way down from living near Harley Street to this.

When we needed water we had to carry it from a communal area inside the building on the ground floor. The communal area consisted of six water taps and sinks, three toilets, but no bathrooms. It had a smell that even today I still find hard to explain. I can remember the sound of dripping taps, mixed with constant shouting emanating from other flats.

Winter had arrived and we only had a small electric fire we had brought with us. It heated the tiny room OK, but with a young child we were constantly on guard in case he went near it. We bought a small, second-hand, two-plate electric tabletop cooker but we didn't have a table to put it on.

We had to take it in turns to sleep, but if we did ever sleep together, we had to top and tail – it was like living in Victorian times, like a prison with an open door. Cary never batted an eyelid; he remained a happy little soul.

Years later, I was swapping stories with the steward of a club in south Wales who had previously lived in London, and he asked me where I had been based. I started running down the list, but when I mentioned Somers Town, he stopped me. 'Not many people have heard of Somers Town,' he said. He went on to tell me about his own bad experience of Somers Town; he was attacked by someone in a pub but managed to flee. I shall never forget his words: 'Somers Town in those days made the Gorbals in Glasgow look like a holiday camp.' I still have the oval brass key ring engraved with our room number and the name 'Polygon Buildings'. Later, when I became a little more successful, I had it coated to stop it tarnishing, and wore it on a chain around my neck as a reminder for, whenever I was down, that things couldn't be worse than those days in Polygon Buildings!

Back then we were living on an average of two shillings and sixpence a day. I didn't know how long we could survive. If it wasn't for Irene helping out we couldn't have made it through.

But after a few months our luck began to change, if you could call it luck! We were offered two rooms on the first floor, with a fireplace. This could accommodate a smokeless coal burning fire. Then one day, rather unexpectedly, Mimi received a letter. It said that she had been awarded two thousand pounds for the accident that had ruined her dancing career. The equivalent in today's money would be around twenty-two thousand pounds. She jumped for joy, but the jubilation soon vanished when she read further. She would not be able to claim the money until she was twenty-one; that would not be until August 1968. She managed to find out, through her lawyer, that if she went before a judge at a special hearing, she might be able to get an advance payment owing to the difficulties she had been through and her loss of work. In the coming years, she made many appearances before the judge, each time receiving advances. Out of her first advance, she loaned me twenty-five pounds to put towards buying a car: a white mini which I desperately needed to transport my guitar, amplifier and speakers. Her subsequent advances were usually spent in Bond Street, either on handbags, shoes, or clothes. Then, by the middle of April 1967, she found she was pregnant again. By the time she was twenty-one, there was hardly any money left.

— CHAPTER FIFTEEN —

Johnny Dee

One afternoon, I was sitting in the *Gioconda* café drinking coffee, feeling despondent and depressed because Mimi's and my relationship was deteriorating. Mimi's leg had healed and she was working once again, but we still couldn't get enough money together to pull us out of our rut. Life seemed to be constantly dragging us down. The advanced payments from her court case were being squandered. In hindsight, they should have been used to lift us out of our dreadful situation, but Mimi thought she was entitled to some pleasure after suffering so much. Maybe not the right decision.

It was quiet in the café that afternoon. There were no musicians around. I had never seen it so dead. I was just finishing my coffee and getting ready to leave when the door opened and in walked this guy who looked like a film star. He was around five foot ten or eleven, deeply suntanned, had long jet-black hair with a fringe, and wore a three-quarter length fitted snakeskin jacket and a shirt the likes of which I had never seen before. The shirt was a lilac colour. It had a short turned up collar with a double row of black satin-like string threaded through. The front of the shirt had two white, embroidered panels down each side of his chest, and running horizontally through them were what I thought was bone, but later discovered was just material that looked like bone. He also wore black trousers and what looked like snakeskin boots. It was like something you would see a Native American wearing. This was the '60s and I had seen some great and unusual looking outfits around Carnaby Street, but this guy was something else. He stood out, even in those days! On the right hand wall of the *Gioconda* were framed photographs of the pop stars that had one time or another frequented the place. He walked over, removed the centre photograph, took the one from the far right-hand side, and replaced it with the one he had taken from the centre.

'That's where that should be,' he pronounced. He was strutting around as if he owned the place. He went up to the counter, ordered a coffee and sat on the opposite side of the café. I looked up at the wall and saw that he had replaced the middle photograph with one of himself. He sat there thumbing through some documents whilst drinking his coffee, humming quietly to himself. I looked at him and thought, *Who the hell does he think he is?* He certainly wasn't a famous face; I'd have seen him around the place if he were. I was on my feet and just about to leave when he turned to me and said, 'How's things?'

'OK,' I replied.

He asked me if I was a muso (slang for a musician). I told him I was and asked him what he did for a living. He told me he was a singer/songwriter and had just returned from Germany. He told me that had been one-half of the male/female duo *Adam & Eve*. They were stars in Germany and had sold over nine million records. He also mentioned that he had written 'Don't Bring Me Down' for *The Pretty Things*, which had reached number 10 in the charts in 1964 (in 1973 David Bowie would also release 'Don't Bring Me Down' on his album *Pin Ups*).

I soon forgot my misgivings – we got on like a house on fire! His name was Johnny Dee and he had been a road manager for a band, but writing that hit song had changed his life. He told me he had a meeting with a few song publishers in half an hour, and said that maybe we could meet up the following day, as he might be able to put some work my way. So we arranged to meet in the *Gioconda* the following afternoon. It was the start of a friendship, and later a business partnership, that would last for just four years but would seem like a lifetime. In those four years, I would learn more about the music business than I could ever have imagined.

Unexpectedly, however, the following afternoon I had a session booked at Central Sound, the recording studio located in the basement next to the *Gioconda*. A fellow musician rang me that morning to book it. Later that afternoon, mid-session, I popped up to the café. John was sitting talking with two people. As I arrived at his table, he introduced me to them. They were songwriters: John Carter and Ken Lewis. John told me that they had written *Herman's Hermits*' hit 'Can't You Hear My Heartbeat'. I was impressed. It had just reached number two in the American charts.

When I mentioned that I had to get back to the recording studio, John said he would like to come with me to hear what we were recording. I was tried to put him off, telling him that those paying for the session would probably not appreciate it. It was quite true – producers didn't want strangers listening in the studio – and I didn't want to be known as someone who would do such a thing. I might not get paid. I might not get booked again. John was having none of it. He just barged down the stairs taking no notice of what I was saying. As he entered the studio everyone turned and stared in amazement. They all seemed to know him. They were shaking his hand, treating him like a star, asking where he had been and what he'd been up to. The producer turned to me and said, 'I had no idea you knew John!'

Before I could open my mouth, John chirped in, 'Yeah, I know Rog. He's a great musician.' As he said it he looked over to me with a wry grin on his face, as if to say, *I told you I was somebody*. He sat in on the session and, when we had finished, praised the producer, saying it could be a big hit. As we were packing our instruments away, he announced that he was forming a band and asked me if I wanted to be the bass player. I told him I would need a better amplifier and bigger speakers. He replied, 'No bother, you can have as many amplifiers and speakers as you like.'

I decided to leave my bass in the studio and headed with John and the other musicians to *The Ship* in Wardour Street for a few beers. After a couple of drinks the other musicians left, so I decided myself to drink up and head for home. But John had other ideas. He mentioned that a club had just opened between *The Ship* and *The Marquee*. It was called *La Chasse*, and it was the in place for all the top bands, musicians and singers. 'We'll row ourselves in,' he joked. That saying would become our motto. We would row ourselves in everywhere, from record companies, to clubs, to parties. I told him I didn't have any money. I wasn't going to spend the session money I had just earned on drinks at

La Chasse. 'Don't worry about money, let's go,' was his reply.

La Chasse was located at 100 Wardour Street, above a betting office. Walking up the creaking steps to the club, I thought to myself, *This is going to be a load of crap!* It was like walking up the stairs of my grandmother's terraced house back in Wales. I'm not saying my grandmother's house was a load of crap. I'm just saying it wouldn't have made a good club. Turning right on to the landing there was a door straight ahead of us. It looked like the door to someone's flat. John knocked hard and someone opened it. I couldn't see who. John just stormed through announcing, 'Johnny Dee.'

I followed closely behind, adding, 'Yeah, that's Johnny.' This so-called 'in club' was just one room, no bigger than an average-sized family sitting room. At a push, it could probably have fitted twenty-five people standing, possibly thirty if you didn't want to move. There were only four or five people there at the time; they were standing drinking at the far side of the bar. John walked straight to the bar. 'Two Bourbons and cola with ice,' he requested, stretching his hand out to the barman. 'I'm John, and this is Roger.'

The barman replied, 'I'm Jack and I'm the owner. Are you a member?'

'I am now,' fired back John.

I thought, no way is he going to get away with this. Indeed, Jack was just opening his mouth when a guy came over from the other side of the bar and cut him off. 'It's OK, Jack. John's a songwriter. He's had a few hit records.' As he was saying this, I realised I recognised the guy: he was a musician by the name of Long John Baldry, a great blues singer who actually gave Rod Stewart his first break and would, later that year, have a number one in the charts with 'Let the Heartaches Begin'. I was introduced to Jack, and for the next few years, *La Chasse* was to become one of my favourite hangouts.

I recruited some good musicians for John's band and we started rehearsals above a pub in Kings Cross. To get to the pub, you had to pass a chapel where, straddled across the front of the building, was a large banner with the words 'God Is Love' written across it. In 1969, John would write a poem called 'God Is Love', turn it into a song, and it would be my first solo single on Deram Records, which was part of the Decca group.

We rehearsed many of John's original songs, some of which I thought had real hit potential. He was hoping to clinch a recording deal with a major record label and get an advance payment from one of the music publisher's in Denmark Street. I was still doing session work at the Central Sound Studio in Denmark Street, and one day John tagged along with me. The session finished early and John asked us if we could record one of his songs in the remaining hour. The other musicians agreed, so we rehearsed the song, recorded it with John singing and were all done and dusted in under an hour. In the '60s, bands such as *The Beatles* and other artistes would record a complete album in a day and they would sell millions.

The following week, I accompanied John to one of the many music publishers in Denmark Street, where he did a deal on the song. The music publisher promised to put him in touch with a few record company executives. I had never seen anyone clinch a deal as quickly as John did. Within a week, he went from recording songs in under an hour, to a twelve month publishing deal to write twenty songs, receiving an advance payment and monthly retainer. So that was how you earned money in the recording industry – he made it look so easy!

It came to John's attention that Eva Gabor was in town. Eva was the younger sister of Zsa Zsa Gabor. Both had made it as film actresses, though Zsa Zsa was far more successful than her younger sister. John disclosed that he had met Eva a while back, I believe in Germany, and he was eager to meet her again. He had found out that she was due to appear on *The Eamonn Andrew's Television Show* the following evening. He was now figuring out a way to get us into the show. Yes us! He was roping me in as well.

Early afternoon the following day, I'm sitting in the *Gioconda* and John appears with the news that he has arranged our entry back stage in exchange for a cash payment.

'How much?' I asked.

'Never mind that. We have to get things organised.'

Our entry to the show ran like clockwork; there was no hassle whatsoever. We were ushered backstage to the green room and were served with drinks. An American singer, Vikki Carr, was on the show that evening, alongside the singing trio *The Bachelors*. Later, someone told me that the playwright Joe Orton had also been on. I can't remember him being there. I think he passed away later that year.

John was continually looking around the room, anticipating Eva's entrance. I asked him why he was so obsessed in meeting Eva again.

'It's not an obsession,' he said. 'I just like her. But it's her sister I fancy.' He meant Zsa Zsa. 'And if I can't have her, she's the next best thing.'

He's taking his chance here, I thought. Eva could have any amount of minders with her. 'If you want to pull a bird, why don't you go down one of the clubs?' I asked.

'I don't want any bird. I want her. She's the next best thing to Zsa Zsa,' he replied.

I was just about to announce I was going to the pub when John's face lit up. Eva had made her entrance. I must admit she was a good-looking woman, very similar in looks to her sister Zsa Zsa. John nervously waited, while she settled in, then he was off, over to introduce himself. I stayed put. Stuff that! I could see a few heavies lurking in the background, and a man, who I thought looked like the late film actor Clark Gable, had accompanied Eva into the room. I watched as John babbled on. I couldn't hear what was being said but Eva began to smile; it was either something John had said or she might have had a touch of wind. After six or seven minutes John returned in a self-congratulatory mood. He said that we should go in to watch the show. I responded that we should find a pub and call back later. John was adamant that he was going to watch the show. I was adamant that I wasn't going to. I told him I would wait for half an hour and then he would find me in the nearest pub. He returned around twenty minutes later, saying, 'C'mon let's find a pub, it's getting boring in there.'

We found the nearest pub and started chatting to a couple of Swedish girls who were over here working. 'We're in here,' he whispered to me.

'You might be, but I'm not,' I replied.

He asked what was wrong with me. I told him my relationship with Mimi was deteriorating and I was not going to add to it with a one night stand. 'She won't know,' he said.

'No, but I will.'

He started buying rounds, and was just in the middle of making arrangements with the girls to see them later at one of the clubs, when he looked up at the clock and realised the show must have finished. It was a mad rush to get back to the green room, with John exclaiming that I should have reminded him of the time.

As we dashed back to the stage door, Eva was just getting into the back of a limousine, followed by the man who looked like Clark Gable. Someone told me later that it was her husband, Richard. John just charged in after them; admittedly, he was a bit pissed by then. As soon as he was in the car he was out again, landing on his arse at the side of the road as it sped off. I walked over, looked down at him and said, 'It'll have to be her sister then.' That went down like a deck hand on a submarine.

'C'mon let's get down the club,' he grumbled.

One of John's contacts had set up a meeting with a music executive from the USA. The meeting was to be at the Hilton Hotel in Park Lane, and John wanted me to go along with him, in his words 'To suss the guy out.' Our contact claimed to be the ex-lawyer of the country recording artist and film star Tex Ritter, who's most famous song was 'High Noon', taken from the film of the same name. The deal was that he would finance the recordings of John's original songs then get them released in the USA. He told us he had contacts with many of the major companies and mentioned Challenge Records, which at one time had been owned by another famous country singer and movie star, Gene Autry. I wanted to know why we couldn't record in the States as well as releasing them there. He said that he had listened to the sound of our recordings, the ones we had done in under an hour, was impressed with the sound quality and production, and wanted us to carry on recording at the same studio.

John later said, 'Who are we to argue as long as he comes up with the money. I don't care where we record.' And once again he made it look so easy. True to his word, the executive's advance came through and we started recording. Over the next week we recorded the songs to a reasonable standard, and found that we had enough money left to hit the clubs for the next few nights, maybe weeks. A short while later we were informed that the first two songs were to be released by Challenge Records in the USA.

I started working with a great little band – not every night, just occasionally – through a musician I had met at a recording session with John. I had money coming in from the band, from my studio work and, for the first time, I was now getting a small cut of advance payments from me and John's outfit as well. John and I were still rehearsing together and, after every rehearsal, John would want to hit the town. It would normally be the same routine: a pub first, then onto *La Chasse* before finishing up at a nightclub. I would always check if everything was OK for Irene to babysit, and off we'd go. After one hard day's rehearsal, when we got to *La Chasse*, it was packed. There was hardly enough room to raise your glass. The first person I spotted was Reggie Dwight (soon to change his name to Elton John). I had, not so long back, with two other musicians, worked on a recording session with him for Dick James Music. Dick himself had once been a singer and his most famous song was 'Robin Hood' from the television series *The Adventures of Robin Hood*. He was now a music publisher and administered Northern Songs, the company set up by *The Beatles* manager Brian Epstein, together with John Lennon and Paul McCartney. George Harrison and Ringo Starr were also signed to Northern Songs. Dick James's son, Stephen, ran their recording studio. In 1969, Dick James sold Northern Songs for a large profit and *The Beatles* felt betrayed; he had sold their songs without informing them.

I introduced John, who then proceeded to tell Reggie how big he had been in Germany, selling millions of records. Reggie already knew. I assumed that David Bowie, another regular at the club, had told him. David had also worked in Germany, under the name Davy Jones, and had released 'The Laughing Gnome' earlier in the year, though it had failed to get into the charts. An album followed but met the same fate. It would still be two years until he had his first big hit with 'Space Oddity'. I used to see David now and again around the West End and in the *Gioconda*. I had been offered an audition for a band he was forming called *The Buzz*. The auditions were at *The Marquee Club* and I was more or less promised the job – all I had to do was turn up. I didn't turn up though. David was virtually unknown at the time and I didn't want to leave the band I had recently joined. We had a great sound and not only was I playing bass, but I was taking the lead vocals on most of the numbers. We thought we were going places, but we didn't and, of course, David did!

At some point that evening, John Banks came over and asked me for a shilling to get home. John had been the original drummer with the top Liverpool band, *The Merseybeats*, though since their break-up, he had been a jobbing drummer, getting work wherever he could. I had wanted John for the recording sessions with Johnny Dee, but unfortunately, the other musicians came as a package, and this included their drummer. John told me that evening that he was off to Israel with his girlfriend. I am not sure if they went as I never saw him again, though I do know that John Banks passed away in 1988.

Another familiar face at *La Chasse* was Tony Stratton-Smith. He was chairman of the independent record label Charisma Records. Then there was Jon Anderson, who went onto form the band *Yes*. Jack Barrie, who eventually ended up running the club, gave him a job working behind the bar. I would always ask Jon to slip me a free drink but he never did. John Dee always used to say, 'He'll never make it with that squeaky voice of his.' He was wrong, of course. Within a year or so *Yes* had become one of the biggest bands in the country.

Johnny Dee, meanwhile, was splashing his money around, buying drinks for everyone; he was really going to town. His drink was bourbon and cola. I was used to drinking beer, but he had won me round by telling me that as bourbon was made from potatoes, it would not give you a hangover.

Someone at the club mentioned they were going to the

Bag O'Nails. This was one of the in clubs in London at the time, and had been known to be frequented by *The Beatles*. So true to our motto we tagged along and rowed ourselves in. On the way John boasted about how he knew *The Beatles* – he had met them on numerous occasions at the *Scotch of St James Club*. *The Scotch of St James Club*, together with the *Ad Lib Club* had been a haunt of *The Beatles*, but new clubs such as *The Bag O'Nails*, *The Speakeasy*, *La Valbonne* (known as *The Valbonne*) and the *Cromwellian* were taking over.

When we arrived at *The Bag O'Nails* in Kingley Street a hatch in the door opened. It was like one of those American gangster movies. Someone looked us up and down, obviously knew the person we were with and in we went. In the weeks that followed, we visited most of the in clubs in London. It was around this time that I met Tom Jones again; he was entering the *Cromwellian* club in Cromwell Road as we were about to leave. He had made it by then: Tommy Scott was no more; he was now definitively Tom Jones. He asked what I had been up to. I told him briefly and he said if I ever needed any help, I was to get in touch through his management.

One night we attended a private party at the *La Valbonne* club. *La Valbonne* was situated in Kingly Street, parallel to Carnaby Street, and was a lovely club. What stood out was that it had its own swimming pool on the dance floor. There were the usual crowd of record executives and pop stars present. I remember a magician going from table to table performing card tricks. He would also read tarot cards. When he got to our table, he started to perform one of his tricks and John stopped him in his tracks. He told him to forget the card tricks and to cut straight to the tarot readings.

The magician told John that he had been living abroad and had returned to live in this country. This was correct. He also said that John would be successful in his chosen career and would marry and move to America. John was pumping the magician, asking if he would continue to be successful in America. The magician said that was all he could tell him, but John was becoming agitated. In the end, the magician stormed off in a huff without reading the cards for me. We knocked back a few – in fact, more than a few – free drinks, then hit another club.

Appearing at the next club was a young and upcoming singer. Someone on the next table to us informed us that his name was David Essex. I had never heard of him and neither had John. I didn't take much notice as his band sounded run of the mill, but John commented that he looked great and sang well, adding he had just the song he could record.

'I thought we were doing that one,' I said.

Between songs, John meandered over to speak to David. I shouted, 'Let the poor man finish his set,' but John was having none of it. This was typical of John; nothing got in his way. He was never in awe of the big stars we met. From a distance I watched as John tried to explain the song to David, his arms flapping around. The audience were getting impatient. Raised voices were heard, demanding that the music start again. John eventually ambled back to the table, looking around at the punters as if to say, 'You can put the music back on now. I've finished what I had to do.' He told me that David had agreed to possibly do the song and had asked John to speak to him after they had finished the set.

Unfortunately we got totally hammered that night. I do remember meeting four German girls. John knew one of them; he said she used to work at a recording company in Frankfurt and, of course, he spoke fluent German, so they got on like a house on fire. I suggested going to *The Speakeasy Club* in Margaret Street, not far from Oxford Circus. It was small but had a great atmosphere. When it opened in late '66 it was an instant success – everyone who was anyone ended up at *The Speakeasy*. John didn't want to play ball; he was happy speaking German to the girls.

'What about David?' I said.

'What David?' he replied

'Essex,' I said.

'He left a while ago.'

'Yeah, to *The Speakeasy*.'

That was it. We were off, with four girls in tow. As we entered the club John spotted David. I breathed a sigh of relief – I'd had no idea where he had got to! John turned to me and said, 'That's what I like about you. You're always on the ball. That's why we work well together.'

John ultimately failed in his pursuance of David Essex, but he was now pulling more money from record companies, publishers and businessmen than ever, and he wanted me by his side twenty-four seven. We worked well together, especially at meetings, bouncing off each other. It was like a sixth sense between us. But although it was great meeting everyone in the recording business, from the session musicians to the so-called stars, I was beginning to feel like I was becoming his clone. I was earning, but not getting my fair share. John didn't want to give me a bigger cut of the advances because he thought I would go off and do my own thing. And if I pushed it too far I might well have ended up with nothing. At least something was better than nothing. The money allowed me to stay with my band and we were getting a few more gigs. I didn't want to finish with them. The clubbing was great and I enjoyed meeting many famous and influential people, but I wanted to get out there and perform myself.

— CHAPTER SIXTEEN—

Meeting the Krays

It was getting near to the birth of my daughter, Sasha, and so I eased off on the nights out and concentrated on earning some extra money. I also took a part-time job, three days a week, with a maintenance company. John thought I was nuts, but at least we would still have four days and nights working and socialising together. The money I earned for the three days, plus part of the money I earned with John, would go straight into the home finances.

It was through the maintenance job that I came to meet Ned Sherrin. The agency sent us to do a job at his home in Chelsea. Ned was the man behind *That Was The Week That Was*, which, at the time was one of the most successful shows on British television, launching the careers of the likes of David Frost, John Cleese, Peter Cook, Willie Rushton, Frankie Howard, Eric Sykes, Bernard Levin, Millicent Martin and many more. Ned also produced around ten films, including *Girl Smugglers*, *Up Pompeii*, and *Up The Front*. Ned greeted us at the door and showed us around the house, telling us what work he needed doing. It was a nice medium-sized terraced house in Bywater Street, Chelsea, consisting of two top floor bedrooms, a ground floor lounge, and a basement which housed the kitchen and bathroom. Ned's secretary, Isabel, used the kitchen table as a desk; she was typing madly away as we entered.

We got chatting to Ned in our break. He told us he was casting for a film called *The Virgin Soldiers*. I remembered that the author of the book *The Virgin Soldiers*, Leslie Thomas, was Welsh, and told Ned that I too was from Wales. I also explained that I was a musician and was only working for the agency to earn some extra money. He said that he had already auditioned David Bowie for a small part in the film, but that he had found his strange quality too elusive to capture on screen. However, he did give him a crowd part, for which he would have to have his hair cut military-style. If you watch the film, Bowie is the person being pushed out from behind the bar. Ned had also offered Mick Jagger a part in the film, but Mick didn't think it was right for him.

The next morning we were greeted by a stream of actors queuing from outside and through the hallway, all waiting to be auditioned by Ned and associates in his lounge. The queue seemed never-ending. In my coffee breaks in the kitchen Isabel would try to persuade me to audition for a part. 'You've got nothing to lose and everything to gain,' she would tell me. However, it was no use; I was too shy in those days. Give me a bass or a guitar and I would come alive, but acting, now that was different.

I worked for Ned intermittently for three to four months. He was always very courteous and helpful, suggesting I should get in touch with a few music business agents he knew, and giving me contacts to ring. Eventually I did call but unfortunately they were looking for musicians who could read music scores. I was too slow at reading the dots so I never attended the auditions.

*

My daughter, Sasha, was born December 1967 at the University Hospital in London. Sasha was fair, more my complexion. And a little more fiery than Cary. We were still living at Polygon Buildings in Somers Town and the living conditions were now putting a severe strain on our relationship – if you could have called it a relationship at that stage. We never seemed to have enough money to get out of the rut.

Soon after, Mimi started work at Bertie Green's *Astor Club* in Berkeley Square. In the '60s *The Astor* was a first-class cabaret venue. It boasted top line performers like Shirley Bassey and Engelbert Humperdinck, and audiences consisted mainly of the rich, famous and criminal element – sprinkled, on occasion, with lesser-known royalty.

In 1965 I had auditioned at *The Astor* after meeting John Maloney at one of our rehearsals. He was carrying out repairs to our building and during a break we got talking. John had been part of a double act working the cabaret circuit, but had to change jobs when the duo had split. He told me that he was looking to get back into show business. He liked my singing and asked if I would do a few rehearsals with him. I agreed and, a few days later, we started the rehearsals in a pub in Romford.

Our voices blended really well and, after a few weeks, we had enough numbers for a cabaret spot. We went to the Gaston and Andre agency and auditioned for them acoustically. They liked us, and a few days later, we were performing at a nightclub in Cambridge, followed by a few appearances in London restaurants. Someone must have been impressed, because that's when we secured our audition at *The Astor*. With the Freddie Mills experience fresh in my memory at the time, I was quite reticent. John, on the other hand, was eager to press ahead and do it. After much persuasion, I said yes.

We did an afternoon audition at *The Astor*. We were on our own: no other musicians, just an acoustic set. We did five audition songs in front of two guys and, surprisingly, I thought it went well. Better than I had expected! Our voices blended well and our harmonies sounded as good as *The Everley Brothers*. The guys asked us for some time to make up their minds, and invited us to return later that evening and check out the club.

When we returned that evening it looked completely different. With the lighting, the glitz and the band playing, we just sat there, our backs against the wall, soaking up the atmosphere. Within minutes we were joined by the same guys who had auditioned us earlier that day. They ordered us a free drink and explained that they would see us later.

Just as they were about to introduce the first singer on stage, John turned to me and said, 'Don't look now, but the Kray twins are in. They're walking this way!' For a second, I didn't register what he was saying. I thought he was talking about a double act – well, I suppose they were in a way.

They were a lot shorter than I imagined. Having only seen their photographs in the newspapers, I thought that they would be over six feet in height, but they were around 5 five foot seven to five foot eight. They were accompanied by two women: very glam, dolly bird types. They walked over and sat at a large table next but one to us. I kept looking over out of the corner of my eye; the Krays seemed to be enjoying the show and even clapped after one of the numbers. I must admit they did have a presence about them.

Even if I hadn't known they were the Kray twins, they would have still had that presence; I don't know what it is, but some people have it and some don't. We sat and watched the singer, who was excellent. He had a powerful Welsh-tinged voice; he could have put the microphone down and you would still have heard him above the band. I wish I could remember his name. I do remember he had a surname usually associated with a first name – like Cliff Richard: two first names. Afterwards, the two guys who had auditioned us came back to our table and, as they sat down, Ron and Reggie Kray began to talk to them. Eventually they got around to talking about the Welsh singer, and I chirped in, 'Yeah, he was great.'

One of the guys explained to the twins, 'These two boys are singers and this one's from Wales.' He went on to introduce us, but he had forgotten our names.

I said, 'I'm Roger and this is John. We're called the James Boys.'

One of the twins replied, 'Sounds like a gang of outlaws. Hope you're as good as your name.' They saw that our glasses were empty and said, 'Do you like brandy?' passing a bottle across the empty table between us. I reached over and took it, thanking them.

I carefully tried to pour only one measure. One of the women laughed, saying, 'Go on don't be afraid. Pour it in!' So I did. John didn't like brandy, so they gave him the whisky bottle and he did the same. The Krays asked us what sort of music we played and how long had we been together as an act – general things, but we were getting on well.

The two guys with us got up, said their goodbyes to the Krays, then said to us, 'When you've got a minute pop around the back and have a chat.'

It wasn't good news. They liked our material and raved about our harmonies, but suggested we get a few more shows under our belts. They went on to say that the door was always open to us and to return in six months for another audition.

As we returned to our table, Ron, Reggie and the others asked what it had all been about. We told them, and they were all very nice, trying to boost our confidence, saying things like, 'Don't worry. You'll get there. Keep trying. Don't be put off. Get another drink down you.' Whatever bad things they may have done they were kindness itself to us. One of them, I can't remember which, even asked us if we were hungry, telling us we could order something to eat. We both refused, not wanting to take advantage of the situation: the drinks were enough.

After another half hour or so, John decided to leave. We arranged to do some rehearsing before the Cambridge gig, and I stayed on to watch the dancers. But I didn't want to outstay my welcome, so after another drink, I thanked everyone and left. It would be two and a half years before I met Reggie Kray again.

John and I fulfilled our bookings, and The Gaston and Andre agency received good reports back from the venues and signed up more work for us. I, on the other hand, wasn't that struck on playing cabaret venues. I wanted to work more with the band. We had recently been offered work in and around the Essex area and I always said that they were my first priority, so it was goodbye to the duo.

In the evenings, I would usually pick Mimi up from *The*

Astor after she had finished work and drive her home, then sometimes head back to the West End with Johnny Dee. It was on once such occasion, when I was waiting for her to finish her shift, that I met Reggie Kray again. There were four other people with him, but Ronnie was not present.

'Hello,' I said as I passed. 'You probably don't remember me, but I met you here before. I was part of a double act. We auditioned in the afternoon, but didn't get the job.'

Reggie looked a bit vague.

'There was a Welsh singer on. You liked him.'

Still no recognition on Reggie's face.

'We were called The James Boys.'

'Oh yeah, I remember. Couldn't forget that name, could I? How are you doing?'

I told him I about my recent recording sessions and about Mimi's dancing career.

'Have a drink with me while you're waiting for her,' said Reggie. So I did, and then another. He was very pleasant, just as he had been the previous time we had met, but his face seemed strained, a little haggard. He continued the conversation I had briefly interrupted. Occasionally one of the fellows prodded his finger on the table, his face stern. Reggie leaned over to mouth something back. I couldn't hear what they were saying; their voices were lowered, and there was music playing. Reggie's head turning from one fellow to another as if he were trying to get a point across. We never spoke again after that. When the show finished, I thanked him and he just smiled and nodded. I wished them all goodnight, picked up Mimi and drove her home. A couple of weeks later I found out that the Kray twins had been arrested.

*

Not long after, I received an urgent message from Johnny Dee, asking me to meet him at *The Ship*. There, he told me that he had signed a major recording deal and he wanted me to co-write some of the material, play on all the recordings, and find the musicians for the project.

'And what will you be doing?' I asked.

'Celebrating,' was his reply. 'And so will you. C'mon were off.'

Just another usual night out really, I thought. We hit nearly every big nightclub in town, John spending money like it was going out of fashion.

At *The Bag O'Nails* we were introduced to Esther and Abi Ofarim. They had just had a number one with 'Cinderella, Rockefella'. After we had all been chatting for a while, John turned to me and said, 'Esther's coming on to you. Go on, get in there. They'll go their separate ways.' He was right, she was coming on to me. Fortunately I spotted a musician friend, made my excuses and went to speak to him. We were having a few drinks and a laugh when suddenly John was in my face. 'Where the fuck have you been? I've been looking for you. We're leaving. We need to hit some more clubs. It's dead here.'

But on the way out John spotted George Harrison and said, 'C'mon, Rog. I know George.'

As we were making our way over, George caught sight of us. 'Johnny Dee,' he shouted across the club. 'Have you written any hits lately?'

'I got loads just waiting to be recorded, haven't I, Rog?' said John as he skipped towards him.

'Yes,' I replied. He definitely had songs, some of them great, but whether they were hits or not, I couldn't be sure.

John introduced me to George who beckoned for us to sit down. As there was only one seat, I was left standing.

George asked me what I did. John interrupted, 'Our Rog is a bass player.'

George jokingly said, 'Leave me your number. You never know!'

Meanwhile, someone on another table called out to John and he went over to talk to them. George beckoned me to sit down and asked, 'I like your psychedelic Cadillac. Was it you driving down Park Lane the other day?'

'How did you know it was ours?' I asked.

'I have my contacts,' he replied with a smile.

The Cadillac in question was a 1963 Cadillac Deville. It was old and not worth much. It had two long fins at the back and was the colours of the rainbow. I must admit it looked a million dollars.

George joked, 'You get the Caddies and paint them. I'll tell everyone I painted them and we'll clean up. Make a fortune!'

He went on to ask what John and I were working on. I told him about John's recording contract and that we were out celebrating. I also told him about the time I worked at *The Cavern* and how Bob Wooler had helped us. George said that Bob had been a very good friend of *The Beatles*. Then I told him about my band and the material we were doing. I must have hit a nerve because it was the music that he was into at the time: old American blues singers, the real vintage stuff. I told him about the time Ken Hope and I were listening to blues on an old Dansette record player. When the needle broke Ken went out to the garden coup, where his father kept a few chickens, brought one in and inserted its beak into the grooves of the record. Remarkably this produced a sound through the chicken's beak. George had never heard anything like it. We were both laughing, and I was really enjoying our chat, when John spoilt everything by returning to the table and announcing, 'Right we're off.'

George looked up. 'Off where?'

'*The Penthouse Club*' said John. 'We've just been invited.'

'Am I invited?' asked George.

'Course you are.'

'Then I don't want to come. I only wanted to know if I would be invited.'

As we said our goodbyes, George turned to me and said, 'We'll have that chat again, next time without being interrupted.'

On our way out John turned to me and said, 'I don't know what the fuck he's on.'

'It was a joke,' I replied.

In the taxi on the way to the club, John kept spouting, 'Row, row, Rog.' We were rowing ourselves into yet another club!

The Penthouse Club was in White Horse Street, which ran from Piccadilly through to Shepherd Street. Bob Guccione, who was from New York and had Sicilian heritage, owned the club. He had opened it in direct competition to Hugh Hefner's *Playboy Club*. Where Hugh Hefner had Playboy Bunnies, Bob Guccione, had Penthouse Pets.

The door staff instantly recognised us and we were led through the club and shown to a table, where drinks were ordered from one of the Penthouse Pets. John was lapping up the attention he was getting from the Pets, while I was beginning to regret coming. To me, the longer we stayed the more boring it became.

John, who was plying a journalist with drinks, turned to me and said, 'We have to keep this guy happy. He can get us a lot of publicity.' It was true the journalist did appear to be well connected. He disappeared for a while and, on his return, beckoned us to follow him. He led us outside the main room, along a short corridor, to where, standing talking to two women, was the owner, Bob Guccione. I instantly recognised him from press photographs, but John had no idea who he was. I had heard that, like Hugh Hefner, Bob Guccione always surrounded himself with beautiful women; that he was smothered in gold chains, one of which had a gold penis hanging from it. That evening, though, he was wearing just one gold chain, a gold ring and a gold wristwatch.

I was into watches at the time – in fact, I still am – so I made a remark – I forget what – about Bob's watch and both he and the women laughed. John had been right about the drinks: the journalist was praising us to the hilt. Bob obviously held the journalist in high esteem. He must have given Bob some good publicity in the past, because after listening to him sing our praises, Bob said that the drinks were on the house for the rest of the evening. In addition, John and I were welcome at the club at any time. Bob would leave our names at the door and, if there was ever any trouble, we were to ask for him personally. On the way back to the table, John turned to me and whispered, 'Now do you want to leave?'

'The hell I do,' I replied. 'We'll stay.'

The next day the journalist from *The Penthouse Club*

telephoned and asked if we would like to meet Scott Walker at his flat. Scott had been one of *The Walker Brothers* but had left the trio to go solo and was now on the lookout for new material to record. He was one of my favourite singers and had enjoyed huge success with hits such as 'The Sun Ain't Gonna Shine (Anymore)' and 'Make It Easy On Yourself'. He had been one of two acts I had seen in Britain who could stir up as much frenzy with the girls as *The Beatles* could; the other was the singer P J Proby. *The Walker Brothers* were to reform in 1975, but for now, Scott was a solo singer.

John was all for letting Scott use some of our songs. I, on the other hand, wasn't sure if it was a good idea. We were on a roll and needed the songs, but I could see how John's mind was working. If Scott decided to recorded them, then it would be more recognition and royalties for John.

We arrived at Scott's flat late that afternoon. A man answered the door, beckoned us in, guided us through into the lounge and said, 'Wait here.' It was dark in the lounge. I could barely see but for a few gleams of light coming through a gap in the curtains. I thought it was rather strange to be shown into a darkened room and told to wait.

I quipped to John, 'What time does the guy with the fangs arrive?'

'Take no notice,' John replied. 'Scott's a bit eccentric.'

After three or four minutes there was still no sign of the guy. 'Maybe he's gone back to his coffin.' I joked. 'Oh no, they only do that when it's light.'

John was halfway through telling me to shut up when a voice from behind us pronounced, 'Scott will see you now!' It frightened me to death. I looked around, but couldn't see its owner 'In there,' the voice continued. *In where*, I thought. I couldn't see a bloody thing. I groped after John and he led me to a door through to another room, also in near complete darkness.

'Scott?' John said.

'Yeah,' came a voice from the darkness.

'Hi, it's Johnny Dee and my friend Roger.'

'Hi man, how are you doing?'

It sounded like the voice was coming from the back of the room, but I couldn't be sure.

I leant towards John and whispered, 'Where the fuck is he?'

'Shut up,' John hissed, grabbing my arm.

'Are we sure it's him?' I persisted. 'It could be anyone.'

John tightened his grip on my arm. 'Shut the fuck up.'

'What's going on, man?' the voice came from the darkness came again.

'Nothing,' replied John. 'Roger was just telling me to get on with it and play the songs.'

'How many songs are there?' the voice came again, louder now – closer.

'Fuck me, he's moved. Where is he?' I whispered. John tried to put his hand up to my mouth but in the darkness missed, one of his fingers prodding my eye. I let out a roar, 'Fucking hell, what are doing?'

'Leave them on the table in the lounge,' replied Scott with a raised voice.

Once we were outside, I broke down laughing. John was furious, ranting on about how I could have blown it, how unprofessional I was, and how I had probably messed up his big chance.

'But how do we know it's Scott,' I asked. 'It could have been anyone.'

John told me that he had known him a few years ago, and it had definitely been him. I must admit it did sound like his voice but I was still unsure. Someone told us later that Scott was suffering from depression. Had I known this at the time I certainly wouldn't have laughed at the situation.

Around this time, we became friendly with actress Susan Shaw. Susan was an English film actress who had appeared in over twenty films between the years of 1946 and 1963, including *London Town, The Good Die Young, Carry On Nurse, Waterfront, The Switch*, as well as the three films about the Huggetts, which were very popular in those days. She had been married to Bonar Colleano a well-known film actor of the day but Bonar had been killed in a traffic accident in 1958 and I know that Susan never got over his death; she retired from the acting profession in 1963. We would visit Susan at her flat from time to time. She had become interested in art and I thought some of her paintings were very good. She also liked a few drinks, and unfortunately the alcohol eventually won. Susan would die of cirrhosis of the liver in 1978 aged just forty-nine.

Daytime was spent recording new material with John, and at night, we were hitting the London clubs. My relationship with Mimi had virtually finished at that point and, although we were still living together, we were each going our separate ways. Consequently John and I were spending more and more time at *The Penthouse*. John would always say that you could find a better class of women there.

He was also interested in one of the Penthouse Pets – well, in fact, all of them. I was getting very concerned because I noticed that John had started signing for drinks. I told him that if we carried on like this we were going to be in a lot of debt. His reply was always, 'Don't worry, we'll pull another advance soon and pay it off.'

But as time went on, I could see that things were getting out of hand. One evening in particular he had racked up a huge bill and was still buying drinks for anyone who sat with us. John had spoken to Bob Guccione and told him he was waiting for advance payment and, as soon as he received it, the bill would be paid. Bob accepted his explanation, but we both knew that if we didn't pay in the next couple of days we were in big trouble.

I would often see Viv Prince around the West End. Viv was the drummer in *The Pretty Things*, the same band that in 1964 had recorded John Dee's song 'Don't Bring Me Down'. Viv had been, without doubt, the first extrovert drummer in the rock and pop business. Keith Moon, drummer with *The Who*, idolised him, and while Keith eventually went on to become even more extrovert, Viv was the first – the original, so to say. Viv was now fronting a club in the West End, not very far from *The Ship* and *The Marquee*, called *Knuckles*. I would often visit there. It was a small club located in a cellar, and Viv would stand outside ushering punters down the stairs. I'm not quite sure whether he was a shareholder or not.

On one of my visits, whilst I was eating one of Viv's famous servings of chicken and chips, he came over and asked if I would like to go to a party that evening in Kensington. It was a near end of tour party for a girl trio called *Reparata and the Delrons*, who had had a top twenty hit previously that year with the song 'Captain of Your Ship'. I had been to see them perform at the *Cromwellian Club* in Cromwell Road a few nights earlier, where a trio called *Clouds* had been backing them. John and I had previously used the keyboard player and the drummer from *Clouds* on a single that we had recorded for Pye Records, called 'Take Me Along'. Viv suggested we gatecrash the party.

'Lead the way,' I replied. I was a natural by now, and we rowed ourselves in without a problem. The party was in full swing. Within a few minutes, Viv had acquired drinks for us and, through a musician friend of his, we were introduced to the girls. *Reparata and the Delrons* were three female singers from New York City. Previously they had released 'Whenever a Teenager Cries' and 'Tommy' in the US, but neither had made much of an impact. 'Captain of Your Ship', however, had been a huge European hit and they were now riding on the crest of a wave. One of the three girls took a shine to me. She was the shortest member of the trio, with long brown hair and Italian looks. We hit it off right away. Even though the party went on for most of the night, she never left my side.

We saw each other a few times after the party, but it was nearing the end of their tour, and as their return to America grew nearer, she asked me to go back with her to New York. They would be recording there, and she had plenty of contacts in the music industry that could help promote me. At the time, I was torn. I really didn't know what to do. It could be the start of a new life for me in New York; the scene was really buzzing over there. But what about Mimi and the children? I could stay and carry on working with John, hoping he could pay off the debt we owed *The Penthouse*.

John wasn't very pleased when I told him of my dilemma. He couldn't understand why I would even consider going to New York when things were happening here for us here.

'You've got the pick of any bird in London,' he said, adding that *Reparata and the Delrons* would fizzle out in under a year. Ultimately, I decided to stay. We were recording soon with a record release around the corner, but most importantly, I knew that if I went to America, I might never see the kids again.

John had to borrow money to cover the debt at *The Penthouse*. He never told me where the money came from, but it was probably the criminal element in the West End. Anyway, with the debt cleared, everything went back to normal – for the time being anyway. It wasn't long before Mimi decided to finish dancing. Although she was working in the West End and it seemed very glamorous, the wages were not that good. So instead she applied and acquired a job as a Penthouse Pet. Yes, the same club as we frequented. From the day she started there, I never went back to the club and, as far as I know, neither did John.

After a short spell at *The Penthouse*, she moved on to taking photographs of the celebrities in the nightspots around central London. It was at *The Speakeasy* one evening, while she was taking photographs, that she bumped in to John. I wasn't with him that night and the inevitable happened. They spent the night together in a hotel in King's Cross. John told me about it the next evening, explaining that because Mimi and I were finished he didn't see any harm in it. I confronted Mimi and she said that as I was seeing other girls, why shouldn't she see other fellas. Fair enough, but why John?

For his new recording career John had now changed his name to John Christian Dee. Pye Records released 'Take Me Along' in June 1968 with a big publicity campaign in the music papers, and as it entered the top forty, I found myself hanging onto John's coat tails as it climbed the charts. So I found it odd when, with everything really starting to happening, John suddenly decided he wanted to uproot and head for America. It had not been long since he was telling me I would be a fool to go myself. His reasoning was that as everything was going so well here, we should hit the USA while we were still hot. I thought we should stay and build on what we had, but he was adamant – it was to be the States. So I went along with the idea. After all, he did seem to have the Midas touch and it would only be for a short time whilst we pulled a few deals. I didn't know then, but there was an ulterior motive behind this decision.

— CHAPTER SEVENTEEN —

Running from the Law

We would be flying from Manchester, and so we decided to spend two nights in Liverpool before heading over to the airport. On our arrival, we booked in at the *Ridgeway Hotel*. We were told that it belonged to the mother of the guitarist Paul Ridgeway, who worked with Freddie Starr.

We hit a few clubs and in one of them, *The Cabin Club*, we got talking to DJ Pete Price, who is now a bit of a legend in Liverpool. Pete introduced us to a few people in the music business. Some had heard 'Take Me Along' on the radio and all seemed interested in what we would do next. One said he thought we were nuts heading for America: we should be here promoting the single. I totally agreed with him, but it was too late – the tickets had been booked and we were leaving within the next two days, or so I thought.

A couple of the local girls joined us and John lost no time in chatting them up. One of the girls recognised me from the time I played *The Cavern*. She remarked that I hadn't changed a bit. It was weird; I was the one getting the attention from the girls for once. John walked off in a huff to the bar.

But not for long. He ended up buying drinks for myself and two of the girls, glancing towards me as if to say, *We're in here*. Another musician approached me, who I had previously met at *The Cavern*. He introduced me to yet more musicians and, as the night wore on, I lost contact with John.

Early morning I made my way back to the hotel. On entering our room, I saw John in bed having sex with one of the girls. He casually looked up and said, 'Where were you? The other one's fucked off.'

It didn't put him off his stroke, he just kept banging away. We spent two eventful nights in Liverpool and had a most enjoyable time.

As we arrived at Manchester airport, I noticed John becoming slightly anxious; he kept looking at his watch, then glancing around as if he expected someone to be watching us. I had not seen him like this before and I asked him if he was feeling OK.

'I'm fine,' he replied. But this wasn't the John I knew. Something was terribly wrong. He was growing more nervous by the minute. The time arrived to board the plane, and I could see he was a bag of nerves. We passed through passport control without any problem, but just as we were walking down the corridor towards the exit gate, someone from behind started shouting. We turned around and saw two security men, accompanied by police, running towards us.

'Run!' shouted John, so we did. I had no idea why, but I assumed he was in a lot of trouble.

We burst through the gate and out onto the runway. As we ran, I gasped, 'This is stupid. We have nowhere to run.' We were fast approaching the plane, beyond which the runway seemed to extend for miles. I glanced behind. The security men and police officers were still on our heels. Back in 1968 there wasn't as many security checks to go through as there are today. I dread to think what would have happened to us if we had tried this today.

'This way,' shouted John, turning a sudden left. We were now heading away from the plane towards open space.

'This is pointless,' I shouted. 'We're not going anywhere.' After another twenty-five yards or so, this must have sunk in, as he decided to stop. But he hadn't given up yet. When the police seized us, he uttered those famous words, 'Do you know who I am?'

A police officer replied, 'Yes, we know who you are, Mr Emery.' *Emery* was John's real name. I couldn't help laughing at his predicament.

Later at the police station, I was released. I was told that they could find nothing to arrest me for. Apparently, I had proceeded through passport control legally, and there was no law to say I could not run to the plane. John, however, was not so lucky; he was escorted to Strangeways Prison in Manchester. I was later told that he owed a considerable amount of child maintenance. John never did tell me how many children he had, but the debt had escalated to a considerable amount, somewhere in the region of nine hundred pounds, which would be around nine thousand in today's money. He arranged a loan from his sister who lived in Wickford, Essex, and asked me if I would collect the money for him and return it to the prison.

This is where George comes in. George was the husband of Mimi's friend Sue. Officially, he was a window cleaner but really, at the time, he was into everything. One evening whilst visiting them in their house in Russell Square, London, he asked us if we would like a takeaway curry. We all agreed we would, but rather curiously George then headed up to his pigeon loft, returning with a dead pigeon. 'This should help with the cost of the meal,' he said, before setting off to pick up the food. God knows what meat was in the curry.

George told me that he had met John Christian Dee in the early '60s around the area of the *2i's*. John had got himself into trouble with two local villains, and was about to get himself beaten up, but George had stepped in and saved the day. He also told me that John had been locked up in Pentonville Prison back in the early sixties – this was news to me!

When John and I had decided we were going to America, we had sold the Cadillac to George, who had since put a roof rack on it to hold the ladders he used for his window cleaning work. Can you imagine the sight of a window cleaner arriving to clean your windows in a huge multi-coloured Cadillac with blacked-out windows? He would often get girls banging on the windows shouting, 'Are you one of *The Beatles*?'

I rang George to ask him if he would take me to Wickford to pick up the money from John's sister. Sue answered the phone, and asked where I was. I said Euston. She replied, 'Oh, it's a clear line. You got there quickly!'

'No, not Houston... Euston Station,' I replied.

George agreed to drive me down to Wickford and then back to Manchester. It would be a good craic, he thought, so we left for Wickford in the Cadillac. A few months previously, John had taken me along to Wickford on one of his visits, so I knew exactly where his sister lived. We collected the money and headed for Manchester. Every time we stopped at a service station, the car would attract a lot of attention, with crowds of people gathering wanting to see inside, and asking George just who we were. George invented a story that I was a new singing sensation from America and he had flown me over to perform on some of the top TV programmes – all bullshit, but he loved it, and so did I.

When we arrived at Strangeways it was too late to pay in the money. The offices were closed for the day, and John could not be released until all the money had been paid, so we decided to head for Liverpool, stay at *The Ridgeway* and have a night on the town. We collected John's case, the one he had packed for our trip to America, and at the hotel, I persuaded George to wear one of John's suits. If you can imagine George, who was a bit of a villain, on the short side and stocky with it, in a long jacket with a velvet collar and velvet cuffs, a red ruffle-front shirt and high heeled boots – he looked ridiculous. He said it made him look like a ponce. I don't know why he went along with it, but after tucking up his sleeves, he reluctantly headed out with me to *The Cabin Club*.

As we entered, Pete Price, the DJ, looked George up and down and remarked, 'Ooh, who's your friend?!'

George shot me a dim look. However, we went on to have a good night, returning to the hotel in the early hours of the morning. Around 4am, I was woken by a noise outside in the corridor. I switched the light on in the room. There was no sign of George, so I assumed he had gone out to the loo, which was situated a few doors away. But then

I heard the noise again – a kind of creaking sound, like straining metal – so I decided to check it out. It seemed to be coming from around the main corridor, so I crept along to investigate. As I peered around the corner, I could see through an open door and into one of the alleyways. George was outside, three quarters of the way up a ladder heading towards a window that had been left open on the first floor. I had no idea how he had acquired the ladder, but what he was doing was not on. I tried to attract is attention without shouting out, but he couldn't hear me, so I raised my voice. But just as I did, I heard footsteps coming our way. I waved frantically at George, and he must have caught a glimpse of me because he started making his way down the ladder. I watched from around the corner as the hotel owner emerged from another door, out into the alley, and headed straight for George. 'What the hell do you think you are you doing?' she shouted, as George reached the bottom of the ladder.

George put his finger to his lips. 'Shhh, I think I spotted someone trying to break in. I'm investigating.'

I could not believe she gave him the benefit of the doubt, but she did. It was quick thinking by George, but even so, as he said later, 'She must have been fucking mad to believe that load of crap.'

We arrived at Strangeways the next morning and the prison officers took us into a side room to check who we were. They knew by now that John was in the music business, and they could see the Cadillac parked outside. One of them told us he sang and played guitar in an amateur group. He was speaking to George because he thought, for some reason, that George was John's manager. George began winding him up, telling him he worked on shows like

Opportunity Knocks and other talent and music shows, and that it wasn't good enough just to sing anymore, he had to do more if he wanted to get on in the business. George asked him for a performance. The officer started to sing. I can't remember what song. George then encouraged him to dance too. I could not believe what I was seeing: a prison officer singing, and trying to dance at the same time, in a room near the entrance to Strangeways. I had to turn away, otherwise I would have burst out laughing. George was lapping it up, telling him to dance faster, and saying it wasn't the right song for him, asking him if he knew any other numbers. George didn't know anything about music, but he took the officer's phone number, turned to me, and said, at a volume he knew that the officer would be able to hear, 'I think he's got something.'

It was bad news for John though. The money we had spent the night before, plus our hotel bill, meant that we were short. The maintenance money also rose each day that it wasn't paid. The bottom line was, we did not have enough money left to get him out of prison. They did, at least, allow us to see him, so that we could find a way to raise the extra cash.

When we were ushered into the visitors' area, he went nuts, ranting about how we were spending his sister's money on hotels and drink, and telling us that he was worried that they were going to cut his hair. It was the wrong thing to do: the more John had a go, the more George wound him up, which just added more fuel to the fire. We left, telling John we would try to sort it out by the following day. But when we got back to the Caddy, George turned to me, and said, 'Let the c*** stew.'

So we headed back to Liverpool and the *Ridgeway Hotel*.

The next day I phoned John's sister, explained the situation to her and she sent up the extra money, but not before we had spent another night on the town. John was released, and in his relief, he forgave us right away. After all, we had work to do: everything was paid up, and although we hadn't reached America, we still had plenty of things going for us here.

— CHAPTER EIGHTEEN —

The Small Problem of Meningitis

It was the 1st of November 1968, my twenty-sixth birthday, and I was on my own drinking in *The Ship*. I was reminiscing, thinking how far I had come, from a small terraced house without electricity in a coal mining village in south Wales to *The Cavern*, the *2i's*, a mews cottage near Harley Street, down to the slum of Polygon Buildings and now playing on chart hits and mingling with the stars. It had been like a dream, a 'rollercoaster ride', and it was far from over. I never even noticed the two girls standing next to me ordering drinks.

'Hi,' said one. 'I've seen you with John Christian Dee around the clubs, haven't I?'

I didn't recognise them but they told me that they were a singing duo called Sue and Sunny, and that they were sisters. I hit it off with Sunny straight away. When she found out it was my birthday, they bought me a drink, and we stayed chatting for around half an hour until they had to leave – but not before I had arranged to see Sunny again.

On the day we had arranged, when I walked through the door of the pub where we had agreed to meet, she was in the centre of a crowd, laughing and joking. It wasn't just me who was overwhelmed by her charisma. She really seemed to be going somewhere. When she spotted me she came straight over and said, 'Shall we go?' She said her goodbyes and we left, heading for the nearest restaurant for a snack and a coffee. A few days later Sue and Sunny went to number one in the charts as the backing vocalists on the Joe Cocker single 'With A Little Help From My Friends'.

That evening we ended up back at her parents' house in the suburbs. I was shocked to see a police helmet hanging behind the door. 'Don't take any notice of that', she said. Nothing happened between us that evening; we chatted together about the business and it was all very pleasant. I went out with her once more but after I was incapacitated by a brief period of illness, I never saw her again. In 1969 she became the lead vocalist in the band *Brotherhood Of Man*, and in 1970 sang the vocal on the worldwide hit 'United We Stand'.

My illness hit just as another single was released. For the first time in years, things were going well for me in the music business, but I couldn't appreciate it. I was laid up back at the flat with what I thought was a sore throat and a fever. I'd been plagued by sore throats and tonsillitis throughout my life.

But every day that passed, my throat and the fever seemed to get worse. I was taking Hypon tablets, the strongest painkillers you could buy, so strong, in fact, that they have since been banned – but they didn't seem to help. As the days went by I felt myself deteriorating alarmingly. I could hardly swallow. I would occasionally try a glass of milk, but that would only make me vomit. Then, in the second week, the headaches started. I was now taking the Hypon tablets as if they were sweets. I remember they used to come in little metal tubes, and it was getting harder for me to unscrew the cap. Irene, who was keeping an eye on me, must have realised I was taking too many and called the doctor. He said I had an extremely bad case of tonsillitis, bordering on quinsy, coupled with flu. He left me a prescription for antibiotics. They had no effect whatsoever.

It was coming up to the third week, and I was lying on a mattress in agony. I could hardly breathe, my head was bursting, and I was continually soaked in sweat. I was in so much pain I didn't care if I lived or died. I was trying to make a noise to attract attention, but knew deep down that my pitiable sounds had no chance of being heard. To make things worse, I was now constantly retching, but there was nothing in my stomach to throw up. I dreaded the daylight, my eyes ached so much, and I dreaded the night: I didn't want to die in the darkness. Because I was sweating so much, I would push the cover off me, and then I would feel my sweat go cold over my body as my pyjamas stuck to my skin, and I would have to pull the cover back over again. I could feel the morning sun on my face, the light showing pink through my closed eyelids. I told myself that this was the end. I could not stand much more. I thought my head was going to burst open. After another night of agony, George came to my rescue. He had been passing and decided to call in. He began knocking the door but I couldn't answer. He told me later that he could hear faint moaning sounds coming from my room so he had decided to smash the door open. I vaguely remember him coming over to me and trying to give me some milk to drink, which I immediately threw up. He rushed round to Oakley Square, into the doctors' surgery. He told me later that the doctor had been reluctant to come as he had patients already waiting. 'But I managed to persuade him,' he said. I can only guess how! The doctor immediately called an ambulance and I was taken to Coppetts Wood Hospital in Muswell Hill and put in the isolation unit.

It turned out that I had the worst kind of bacterial meningitis, coupled with glandular fever. They did not know whether I would survive. My parents and family rushed up to London to see me. My mother had seen her fourteen-year-old brother die of bacterial meningitis and knew what the consequences could be. At first, they were not even allowed in, but as time went by, they were permitted to join me provided they wore facemasks. I was still in terrible pain and I remember gripping the metal headboard so tight that, at times, they had difficulty releasing my hands. My only comforts were when they carried out lumbar punctures, draining off fluid from the brain to temporarily ease the pain, and a very kind nurse, originally from the Caribbean, who would sit with me every night during my isolation.

There must have been someone looking out for me. I had been laid up for months but I had survived. When I came out of hospital I weighed under six stone and looked like a POW.

Just before I became ill John and I had been drinking with *The Paper Dolls*, the singer PJ Proby, and the Radio Luxemburg DJ Tony Prince. John and PJ Proby were arguing as to who had sold the most records in Germany. They were practically coming to blows. Eventually things calmed down and I said to John that I thought we should leave. As we stood outside the hotel, waiting for a taxi, a dark red Rolls Royce, driven by a blonde women passed slowly by. John turned to me and announced, 'I'm going to marry her.'

Then one day while I was recuperating, my mother handed me one of the daily papers, saying, 'Don't you know this fellow?' It featured an article on John and read: 'Pop Star John Christian Dee Marries Singer and Socialite Janie Jones.' There was a picture of the couple, arms wrapped around each other. I recognised the woman at once: she was the woman in the Rolls Royce that evening! John had said he would marry her and he had done. God knows how!

I had returned to Wales to spend a few months recuperating, and when I was feeling better, I was in two minds whether I should return to London. Eventually the big city won, again. With a loan from my parents, I bought an old Mini and sprayed it black. It was a bit of a wreck and I wasn't entirely convinced it would make it all the way to London, but it just about managed it. I had arranged to stay at Irene's flat on my return, and while I was there, Mimi and I reconciled. Soon we secured the tenancy of a two bedroom flat in the Regent's Park area. We were back together again – for a while anyway.

— CHAPTER NINETEEN —

Germany Calling... Twice

January 1969 started well. Mimi was working and I got a job in a new band. People even wanted to invest money in us. For the time being, John was forgotten as I concentrated on *my* music.

We were now both making the most of our children, and together we would take them out on a regular basis. We were located just across the road from Regents Park and would go there often for picnics. Both children seemed to look forward to this.

By chance, on a night out, I met the singer Keith Dangerfield, who was managed by the businessman Ted Laskowski. Keith had heard that I had been recording with John Christian Dee and was eager to team up with me. He suggested that I should meet Ted, I agreed, and he arranged for us to meet at his place to discuss our plans. The meeting, when it occurred, wasn't exactly what I had been expecting. Keith explained to Ted that he was owed a substantial amount of money for two songs he had written for a German publishing company. He asked Ted if he would loan him his fare and expenses to collect the money from their offices in Hamburg, and promised that he would repay him on his return. I thought this was a bit of an odd request, but Keith said he didn't have a bank account. It still seemed strange: Keith could have asked the publisher send him a cheque, then Ted could have cashed it for him. Keith suggested to Ted that I should go along with him! This was completely out of the blue. I wasn't too sure about this: I didn't want to get involved – I had met Keith a day earlier, and Ted only a few minutes previously. But surprisingly Ted said seemed to think it was a good idea, so to keep him happy, and because I had never been to Germany, let alone Hamburg, the city where *The Beatles* had cut their teeth, I agreed.

Two days later we arrived in Hamburg and booked ourselves into a small hotel, just off the Reeperbahn. We had our first night on the town, visiting all the old haunts where the British bands had played, and in a club near the Eros centre got chatting to a few girls who we soon found out were prostitutes. They wanted us to go off somewhere to do the deed. I said to one of them, 'We don't pay for it, darling,' to which she reached into her bag and pulled out a small hand pistol! In an instant Keith had grabbed it from her hand. Thankfully one of the bar staff had alerted security and the two girls were escorted out of the building. Apparently most German prostitutes carried these pistols. They were powered by small gas cylinders and fired ball bearings. They were powerful enough to penetrate a London telephone directory and they were available to buy in the local shops, so the prostitutes used them for protection.

The following day Keith headed off to the publishers to collect his money, but when he returned he didn't have the cheque. For the next few days, he would disappear for three or four hours at a time. On his return he would always tell me the same story: that he was chasing up the money, a substantial amount, but the cheque wasn't yet ready. When I asked him 'How much?', he was unable to answer the question. Soon we had spent all the money Ted had advanced us and we had nothing left. I started eating the sugar cubes from the bowl on the table. 'This is stupid,' I said. 'Phone Ted and ask him to send some money. I'll pay him back when we get home.' Rather conveniently, as soon as Ted's money arrived, Keith finally got the cheque.

Back home Ted asked to see the cheque. Keith said it was in a safe place and it would have to go through PRS here before he could get the cash. Ted was adamant. He wanted to see the cheque. Keith explained that it was in a safe place but Ted wouldn't let it go: where was this 'safe place'? How much the cheque was made out for? This went on and on. Finally, Keith came out with the most stupid remark I have ever heard. 'It's in the heel of my boot,' he said. I couldn't believe what I had just heard, and neither could Ted.

'Show me,' Ted shouted.

'It's safe,' came the reply.

'Right, take his boot off, Rog,' ordered Ted, who was now holding Keith down in the chair.

'OK, OK.' Keith stuttered. 'I don't have it on me, but you'll have the money by tomorrow. I promise.' Ted did get his money the next day. Where Keith got it from, I don't know, but Ted seemed satisfied. It was obvious to me, that the whole trip had been a sham on Keith's part. Months later he admitted to me that he had been previously been involved with a girl in Hamburg, and had used the trip to see her. Why the Hell it had been necessary for me to join him I will never know. My best guess is that he had heard some stories about me and John, and wanted somebody to go out on the town with.

Travelling over to Essex one morning I stopped off at a garage to fill up with petrol. As the attendant took my money, she said, 'You look like a pop star. Are you pop star? Who are you?' I don't know what gave it away; perhaps it was the way I was dressed.

'I do a bit in the music business,' I replied.

'Ere, this guy's a pop star,' she shouted to a fellow who was standing at back of the garage. After a brief chat, I returned to my car and found a business card on the passenger seat. It had the name and telephone number of the garage, so I put it in my pocket and drove off. When I returned home later that evening, I looked at the card again and realised that someone had written another telephone number on the back of it, with a message which read: 'I have a great band, please ring me.' So I did, and I got through to a John Morphew. As I had suspected, he wanted me to work to promote his band, promising that I would be well paid for my efforts. He owned a car sales company as well as a garage, and I would be supplied, within reason, with a car of my choice. It was a really tempting offer. Cars had always been a passion of mine, and this guy was handing me one on a plate. But after thinking it over I declined. I didn't want to be indebted to anyone, and for now, my only concern was trying to get my own band a recording deal. I did tell him that I would keep in touch, and that I might be able to help in the future, but after I hung up the phone I thought it unlikely that we would ever speak again. However, I was wrong: I would be contacting John Morphew again sooner than I thought.

I had lost contact with John Christian Dee, but Keith Dangerfield was gradually taking his place. He would constantly telephone me, asking me to join him on one or other of his deals. I was very wary of him since our trip to Hamburg, but he was coming up with a few good offers which I found hard to refuse. In spite of all his faults, he was still a nice guy, and when we did meet up, we always had a good laugh. One day he rang to tell me that Ted had booked a recording session for him at the *RG Jones Studio* in Morden, SW London, and they wanted me to produce it.

I arrived at the studio early the following evening. Why the evening? Keith had told Ted that he could only record at night; apparently his voice was better that way. *Really*, I thought. But they had booked some very good musicians, one of whom I knew, and an hour or so setting up the sound, then we were ready to go. Ted had brought an accountant friend with him, and they were sat behind the sound desk with me as the band ran through the intro. When Keith started singing I saw Ted turn to his friend with a look of despair. I tried to ease his mind, saying it was a great sound and that Keith had written a good song. We could still get a record company interested in it, or re-record the vocal, or even get another singer. Keith wouldn't mind: he'd still get his song-writing royalties. In truth listening back to it today, Keith didn't sound too bad at all.

The following day I decided, armed with the demo disc, to head to Robert Stigwood's office in Mayfair. I had met Robert briefly a few years earlier. Having lost most of his money in a previous venture, he was now riding high again with *The Bee Gees*. As I walked up to reception, I had no idea whether or not he would see me. The receptionist made it clear that I could not see him without an appointment and there was no way I would get an appointment unless I was a record company executive. However, I had learned from John never to take no for an answer. This receptionist was not going to stop me; I was going to row, row myself in. I explained to her that I had flown over from America to record this new single, that I was with Challenge Records in the USA and recording here in England on behalf of Pye Records. I told her I had finished the recordings and would be flying back the next day. I also said that Robert, who I knew from way back, would not be too pleased if I returned to the States without him having heard this record first. She rang through and after explaining the situation, put the phone down and said that Robert would see me. When I entered his office Robert said, 'Oh yes. I've seen you before somewhere.' But he couldn't remember where. After prompting, he said vaguely 'Oh... yes.' I don't think he remembered at all, but I didn't really care. I was in and that's what mattered. He sat in silence, listening to the recording. When it finished he turned to me and said, 'How the hell did you get that drum sound. It's awesome. I have never heard a drum sound on record like it!' He never mentioned anything about the song itself, but it was obvious that he was knocked out by the sound. Perhaps I could recreate it for some of his other artistes? He offered me use of the studio across the road, where I would be under the guidance of a man named Robert Masters. I, of course, had to bring Keith in with me, as it had been his idea in the first place.

When we turned up at the studio Robert Masters gave

us free rein. We had decided to record an album featuring covers of acts from the past. We were calling it *Ghosts*. I still have a demo copy of the album, but I'm not sure if they renamed it when it was released. Keith kept trying to impress Robert with his studio know-how, but he was finding it difficult to remember how we had set up the instruments at the original recording session. In the end he gave up, saying to me, 'You do it.' Towards the end of the first day we managed to recapture the sound, and Robert Masters agreed that it was excellent, particularly the drum sound. However, the following day Keith arrived early and changed the positions of all the microphones. He said he wanted to try a get a new sound, a better sound. I had worked hard the previous day, and Robert Masters had been pleased the way the session was progressing, but now Keith wanted to change it all. I had to rearrange everything, rebalance every instrument; it was all time consuming and I was not a happy chappy.

Two or three days later, Robert Masters returned from one of his meetings with Robert Stigwood and pronounced, 'I have some news for you.'

Keith replied, 'What's that?

'It's not for you, it's for *you*,' he replied, pointing his finger towards me. 'Robert [he meant Robert Stigwood] wants you to fly out to Polydor in Hamburg and work for a while.' Apparently, he was hoping I could show their studio engineers some of my tricks. I didn't know what to say. I had just been given the freedom of the recording studio. Why would I want to go to Germany now? 'You'll love it out there,' he added at my hesitation.

Keith began winding me up, saying, 'Na na na na na.

Who's a scardie cat?' I think he just wanted me out of the way. Robert Masters eventually persuaded me that I should give it a try. He said they needed someone out there with fresh ideas and I couldn't lose anything by going. I made a compromise and said that I would give it three days out there and if I didn't like it, I would be back. I had had enough of people telling me what I should do. They wanted me, so now I was telling them what I was going to do.

I was leaving Keith in complete control of the studio. When I set off that day, he was already slapping stickers for the RSO (Robert Stigwood Organisation) and Abigail (*The Bee Gees*' music label) on blank acetates (blank recording discs). I called in again two days later, just before I was due to leave for the airport. The band was sitting around drinking coffee, while an engineer was busy taking a section of the recording equipment apart. Robert Masters was present and he told me that the sound had been so bad that Keith had complained that there was something wrong with the recording equipment. The band looked over to me and one of them muttered, 'Why don't you stay and get the album finished. We'll tell Robert we need you here.' Meanwhile, Keith was sitting at the recording desk, whistling away to himself like it was all in a day's work.

'When are you off?' he called over.

'Tomorrow,' I replied.

'You don't have to go if you don't want to.'

I thought I could sense a little bit of desperation in his voice. I saw what was going on: the whistling had been for my benefit; Keith had realised that perhaps there was a little more to this production malarkey than he had thought. So I answered, 'I'm looking forward to it now. I can't wait.'

'I was only winding you up. You would be better off staying and finishing this. It might be big.'

'No, you can handle it. Anyway it was through your song that we got ourselves in here.'

In the end, I was out in Hamburg for just under a week. The people at the studio were very nice, and they seemed interested in what I had to show them, but I was still a little at a loss to what was expected of me. Ostensibly, I suppose, I was a kind of producer/consultant, but when I told one of the recording trainees, a guy called Graham, that I could do with earning some extra money, he said that he could introduce me to a music publisher. I told him I didn't have any songs. 'Not to worry,' he said. 'Take your guitar along, stamp your foot on the floor to a marching beat and strum the guitar. Make up some words 'cause the two guys don't speak English very well. The Germans love a marching beat and you'll make some money.'

I was very apprehensive as I stood, guitar in hand, before the two publishers. Graham began chatting away to the two of them in fluent German, and I had no idea what they were talking about. Then he turned to me and said, 'Right! Remember what I told you. Off you go.' I had already written some lyrics, and had had an idea for a tune, so I started. The publishers sat there in silence until I finished the song. They said something to Graham; he turned to me and translated. 'They want to hear another one.'

'Another one?' I blurted out.

'Yeah go on, do the same beat, but change the tune.'

So I did, making the melody up as I went along, and throwing together whatever phrases popped into my head for the lyrics. The publishers were nodding their heads to the beat and smiling. I thought to myself *Bloody Hell, I'm on to a winner here!* They wanted to hear one more, so I changed the beat and the tune slightly and went again. I was now getting good at this, though I couldn't think of any new lyrics – bad English or no bad English, I suspected the Germans would realise if I just started singing the same old things – so I just hummed along. Graham told them I hadn't finished writing the lyrics. They liked what they heard and an advance payment equivalent to fifty pounds was coming my way as soon as I signed the publishing contract. I couldn't believe this! I was struggling to earn money playing in bands, and I had just earned fifty pounds in a half hour by making things up on the spot. Fifty pounds in 1969 was equivalent to around five hundred at today's rate.

The following day Keith telephoned with the news that he had finished at the studio. Things were not going well for him there and they had brought someone else in to finish off the album. He informed me that they were keeping the track I had produced, but otherwise they were starting again. He said he was coming over to Hamburg, so I said, 'Great, I'm coming back to London.' Although things were progressing reasonably well, and I had only been in Hamburg for a few days, I still missed London. Keith said that if I was returning, he would leave the German trip on hold for a while. I finished what I was working on and, a few days later, I was on my way back to London.

— CHAPTER TWENTY —

God Is Love

I had only been back in London a day when I received a telephone call from *The New Musical Express*. Someone had given them my number; at the time I suspected Max Munday. Max was a theatrical agent I used to see now and again around the West End. He was always advising me to get into acting; it would be another string to my bow, he would say. Every time we met he would ask if he could put me up for auditions. I told him that I had never acted before, not unless you counted that one advert for Lyon's Ice cream years ago. But that never seemed to put him off. 'You'd be a natural,' he would say. 'All the Welsh can sing and act.'

I'm not sure where he got this idea from. I suppose the singing part made sense. Welsh singers and bands, such as *Amen Corner* and *The Iveys* (who eventually changed their name to Badfinger), Swansea-born Spencer Davis, Dave Edmunds and of course Tom Jones, were making waves in London at the time. *The Rolling Stones* were even quoted as saying that they were reluctant to play Wales as the standard of our bands was so high!

But who knows where his conviction that we were all great actors came from. And I'm still not sure what his motive behind setting up the interview was, either. But it went well, the interviewer asked me some general questions about the London scene and my own plans. I was just about to leave when the reporter remarked, more to himself than to me, 'Oh well, I have to start all over again now.'

I asked what he meant, and he told me he had another interview in a couple of minutes. I said, jokingly, 'Anyone I know?'

'John Christian Dee and Janie Jones,' he replied. What were the odds? I told the interviewer I had worked with John many times in the past, and that we were good friends but had lost touch with each other. The reporter said I could wait until they arrived and, just as he finished speaking, there they were standing at the door. John was very surprised, but said it was great to see me again. He had tried telephoning, but Mimi had moved out of Polygon Buildings. He introduced me to Janie and, after a brief chat, we exchanged telephone numbers, with John promising to invite me over.

That evening I had arranged to pick Mimi up from work, but I was unfortunately waylaid. I had met an old musician friend of mine and he had introduced me to this guy, a London heavy I shall call Jack. Jack invited us both to a club, somewhere between Tottenham Court Road and Rathbone Place. It was a small club and my musician friend said it was full of villains. After an hour or so it began to fill up. It looked like half of the London underworld was there. I was introduced to a few of them. They all seemed to be fascinated that we were musicians, and it was equally interesting for us listening to their nefarious stories. Jack told us, 'Keep in with this lot and you'll never have any problems. Know what I mean?' We both knew exactly what he meant. They bought us drink after drink, until I realised the time and said I would have to go. Jack said, 'See you again sometime. In *The Ship* maybe?'

By the time I arrived to pick up Mimi, she had left. I drove back to the flat and found the door had been bolted on the inside. I knocked on the door but got no reply, so I began banging on it hard. I thought Irene might have answered, as she was looking after the children, but there was still no reply. I gave it one last knock, I drew about six paces back, took a deep breath, and ran at the door, hitting it with my left shoulder. The door burst open, hitting Mimi, who was just about to unlock it. She fell to the ground and I stumbled over her. I felt awful; luckily she wasn't hurt. She told me later that she had bolted the door because she was annoyed that I hadn't picked her up at the club. Either the door locks were of inferior quality or the bourbon was getting stronger. Our relationship was once again on the decline, but this only made things worse.

A few days later, as I was just about to leave the flat, the phone rang. It was John Dee inviting me over to Janie Jones's house. Janie's house was a modest Georgian-style terrace situated in Campden Hill Road. As I opened the front gate, I couldn't help but notice her dark-red Rolls Royce parked outside. John introduced me to Janie. She was blonde, attractive, down to earth, and made me feel very welcome. Nothing was too much trouble, and if she couldn't help you herself, there was Eric. Eric was Janie's butler. He worked at a law court by day and at Janie's in the evenings and at weekends. Eric was a timid sort of fellow: bald, slim, around five foot nine. He didn't say much, but did exactly what Janie ordered him to do, whether making tea or shopping. She would stamp her foot on the lounge floor and, as if by magic, Eric would appear. Occasionally she would go a little over the top with her orders, and on such times, Eric would always come out with, 'Eee, you're like a bloody Sergeant Major.' But this was always tongue-in-cheek, and I could sense Janie liked him a lot, although at times she didn't show it. Janie had been around the showbiz scene in London for a number of years. She had started working as a cabaret act around the West End, eventually teaming up with her younger sister Valerie and working as a double act. It was while performing in *The Georgian Club* that she had met Eric, who had been down in London on a fortnight's holiday from Southport, where he lived with his mother.

Janie had some chart success in 1966 with the song 'Witches Brew', and at the time had been on the lookout for some new material to record. She had been introduced to John by the singer Long John Baldry. He had apparently told Janie that John was a great songwriter but was on drugs and needed a place to stay. If she let John stay at her house it could benefit both of them. John could write songs and they could split the money. John had played some of his material and Janie thought it was great – so she took a chance on him.

As we sat in the lounge, John played a few recent songs, one of which was called 'God Is Love', inspired by the banner the two of us would always see on our walks to rehearsals. We talked until late. I told him about John Morphew, the car dealer I had recently met who was interested in the music industry. John suggested that we ask John Morphew if he would finance 'God Is Love' – John would give me the song and I could record it as a solo record. I wasn't too sure about recording a religious song. I was into more rock material. But John was enthusiastic about it, saying that it could be big in America. 'You could tour the Bible Belt!' he said. He added that he had heard on the grapevine that Billy Preston was going to release a religious single. 'What have you got to lose?' he asked. 'You'll have a single out on a major label. What have you got now?'

I would have liked to get offended at this, but he was right: I didn't really have anything at the time. I told him I would put it to John Morphew, though for now I said my goodbyes. As I was just standing to go, two glamorous girls showed up. John and Janie introduced me, and as I was leaving John caught my eye and winked at me. 'You'll be back.'

He was right. Not long afterwards I was invited to one of Janie's Friday night parties and I jumped at the chance. Janie's parties were well-known in the entertainment business. Everyone wanted an invite, but it was only the chosen few that got one. The night I arrived Janie told me I had just missed Tom Jones and his manager Gordon Mills. But there were still plenty there. As I made my way through the throng I spotted TV producers; film producers; radio DJs; actors; performers; singers – the likes of Malcolm Roberts, who had had a top ten hit with 'May I Have The Next Dance With You' and was later in the year to have more success with the ballad 'Love is All'; and Paul and Barry Ryan, the brothers whose song 'Eloise', sung by Barry and written by Paul, had been a huge hit the previous year.

Then there were the girls there from *The Penthouse Club*, who throughout the evening people disappeared upstairs with the guests.

There was one girl in particular who stood out – literally: a buxom woman by the name of Zelda Plum. Zelda had been a hostess at one of the clubs where Janie had previously worked. Her party piece was that she would dance naked, her hair piled on top of her head like a beehive, a chinchilla nestled in the middle of it. But this wasn't her only trick; she had quite the repertoire. I will never forget Paul and Barry Ryan's faces during her exhibition of the many uses of a cucumber.

Once they had sufficiently recovered, John introduced me to the two brothers, and we discussed the music scene. I asked them about their mother, Marion Ryan. She had been a famous singer in the fifties and, as they told me, was now with the showbiz millionaire Harold Davison. Harold Davidson controlled most of the American big name acts coming in to the country, including Frank Sinatra. I told Paul and Barry that 'Eloise' was one of my favourite songs – I still think its production is up there with the likes of Phil Spector's 'You've Lost That Loving Feeling' – and Paul offered to play John and me something he had just written. He sat at the piano and performed a lovely song entitled 'I Will Drink the Wine'. Frank Sinatra went on to record it and performed it at the Albert Hall.

Meanwhile, Janie had retired to the kitchen to help Eric with something. A little while later she appeared with a big tray, bellowing, 'Anyone for sandwiches?'

'What's in them?' I asked.

'Salmon and cucumber,' she said with a wicked smile.

I declined her offer.

On my occasional visits to Janie's, some evenings were spent relaxing, having a drink, and watching television. You never knew who might pop round though. One evening, we had just begun to watch a film when there was a knock at the door. Janie answered it and in walked a well-known TV presenter, accompanied by a girl I recognised from *The Penthouse Club*. He apologised for interrupting and made some small talk. While we were talking, the girl slipped upstairs; a little while later, so did the TV presenter. Around forty-five minutes or so later he reappeared, looking a little flustered, accepted a drink from Janie, then left, apologising again for interrupting on his way out. No comment was passed at this, and neither Janie nor John seemed remotely bothered, so I thought nothing of it. At Janie's, apparently, it was just the sort of thing you could expect.

All this was getting a bit too much for Eric alone to handle, however, so Janie was looking for a housekeeper. As chance would have it, Keith had recently rang me to say that Rose, a Scottish girl who had a crush on me, was looking for accommodation. Initially Janie had been looking for someone Swedish: at the time there were hundreds of Swedish, Norwegian, and Dutch girls living in London, mostly working as Au Pairs, and Janie, who always knew what she wanted, had decided on a Swede. I remarked that I didn't know anyone Swedish, but how about a Scottish girl?

'Scotland's close enough!' Janie replied.

The only difficulty, as I explained to Janie, was that Rose had a thing for me. She seemed a nice girl, but I wasn't interested; if she came to work here, things might get awkward. Janie said, 'Leave everything to me. If she wants the job, she won't be bothering you.'

A job in London with accommodation thrown in? Rose leapt at the chance. She arrived for the interview the following afternoon. I was told later her first question was how frequently I would be around.

John, when not writing or playing music, was continually modernising his old Mini. He replaced the seats with the best sports seats money could buy, put in a small television, had the best alloy wheels he could find and installed blacked-out windows. The car was then sprayed British Racing Green, with gold racing stripes running up the bonnet. He found authentic Mini Cooper badges to replace whichever brand had been displayed, and polished them till they gleamed. All this, and it didn't even have a first gear. John could have bought a real Mini Cooper with the money he spent. I never quite understood it.

When John Morphew agreed to put up the money for 'God Is Love', however, John tore himself away from his garage and invited him and his business partner over to Janie's to discuss the deal. We agreed we would record 'God Is Love' as an A-side ourselves, in one of the privately owned recording studios, and then lease it to a major record label. That way, instead of the two and a quarter to two and a half per cent royalties we would receive if we approached a label first, we could get around twelve and a half per cent. With everything agreed, we began to set things in motion.

I was still unsure about recording 'God Is Love'. It just wasn't my type of song. But before I knew it John had recruited Bill Shepherd to write the arrangement. Bill had recently been working with *The Bee Gees* and was organising a small orchestra consisting of violins, cellos, brass section, backing signers plus Big Jim Sullivan on guitar (Jim who would go on to work Las Vegas in Tom Jones's band; was one of the most sought-after guitarists of the London scene; if you wanted a guitarist to really fire up your record, it was a straight choice between Big Jim or Little Jim [Jimmy Page]). The cost was mounting – the studio alone would cost a fortune – but John didn't seem to care. After all, he wasn't paying for anything – it was all was coming out of John Morphew's pocket.

When we were finished with the session, I was far from pleased with the results. I couldn't fault the musicians, but my vocals made me cringe. I wanted to go back into the studio and re-record, but John insisted that I sounded OK and that he would approach Decca with the master tape. Decca liked the song but wanted me to overdub what I can only describe as a choirboy-type voice onto it. For me things were going from bad to worse. I didn't want to sound like a choirboy; I was a rock singer! But Decca promised that if we did things their way, they would be able to get a lot of publicity, so we went back in the studio and re-recorded the voice. I feel this made the song even worse, but the record company, for some reason, agreed to release it on Deram, a subsidiary label of Decca Records. By now I didn't want anything to do with it. I asked if the B and A sides could be switched. The B-side was a song called 'Sister Mimi'. The vocals were not much better; however it was a sing-along type of number so this was less noticeable. Sadly Decca were having none of it. The release date was set for the 11th

July 1969. Mercifully, this was to be under a stage name: R J Hightower.

The reviews for 'God Is Love' were generally good. In particular, David Wigg in the *Daily Express* gave it a glowing report. I can only assume that all the journalists were in the same bar and under the influence at the same time. Decca wanted to do some publicity in Wales for the launch. They thought it would be good to publicise it at a local record shop and get the radio and TV involved. Unfortunately the shop where I used to buy my records in my youth had closed its record section – it was now solely an electrical shop, selling such things as TVs, radios and vacuum cleaners. The nearest record shop or stall still going was situated at the indoor market in Caerphilly. When I was very young, my grandmother would take me shopping there on a Saturday. My grandmother, my Auntie Rene and my cousin Dawn and her husband Bill still lived in Llanbradach, so it would be a bit of a homecoming.

The record stall owner was happy to go ahead with the promotion, and I was told that on the day a big limousine would be hired to drive me through Caerphilly. I had all the latest clothes supplied free by the Take 6 shop in Carnaby Street; in return for modelling them at a photo shoot arranged by Decca, they even allowed me to keep some of them. The photographs from the shoot would eventually feature on billboards around the country. I can remember Ken Hope telling me that every day, on his way to his job on the Treforest industrial estate near Pontypridd, his bus would pass a billboard featuring me dressed in a suit, frilly shirt and Cuban-heeled boots. He said it used to do his head in. He just wanted to wipe the smile off my face. 'But,' he added. 'I couldn't help looking at it every day.' Then the day came when I was replaced by a washing powder advert. Apparently his mate turned to him and said, 'You can relax. He's probably all washed up by now!'

As my limousine approached Caerphilly market, I could hear a live band playing. The music seemed to be coming from up above the market, on the first floor. It brought back so many memories. Otherwise the street was quiet. 'Not many people around,' the driver remarked.

Just inside the entrance to the market there was a banner strung between two stalls. It had my name written across it in huge letters; beneath that, in smaller print, were the words 'God Is Love' and its release date. I walked towards the record stall with great anticipation. There, standing outside the stall, was my auntie Rene and cousin Dawn. Apart from one or two browsing inside the stall, they were the only ones there. I had known not to expect my parents: they were on holiday with my sister. But this I hadn't expected.

'Your hair looks nice,' Dawn said. 'Pity your mother couldn't be here. How long are you staying? I love your record, by the way.'

'I don't think much of it,' a woman browsing butted in. 'They've been playing it all morning. I like up-tempo stuff, I do.'

'Then get upstairs and listen to the rubbish that band's playing,' the shopkeeper bit back. 'They shouldn't be allowed to rehearse while the market's open. I'm going to complain. This is the second time this 'as happened.'

'Is that where everyone's gone?' I asked. 'There's not many here. In fact there's only two.'

'It takes two to tango,' said the browsing woman.

'Then tango off. You haven't bought anything anyway,' the shopkeeper replied.

'You would only get a crowd here if it was Tom Jones or Shirley Bassey,' remarked the woman on her way out. She turned and met my eye. 'Even then you would have to give them something for free.'

I had been brought thoroughly down to earth.

But eventually a small crowd did start to gather and the records began selling. One old fellow who came up and asked me to sign the cover said that he knew my auntie Rene and cousin Dawn. 'But I'll give you a piece of advice boy,' he said. 'I wouldn't dress like that around here.'

Afterwards I went back with my auntie to the house in Llanbradach – the house where I was born – to see my grandmother and have a cup of tea and bite to eat. Lovely, but not exactly rock 'n' roll!

Back in London, John Morphew's band had been renamed *Bulldog Breed* and Louis Farrell from *The Gun* brought in as their new drummer. *The Gun* had previously been in the charts with a song called 'Race With The Devil'. Now *Bulldog Breed* were being signed to Deram. I watched this happen – as I had with so many of those around me at this point – and thought about getting into management myself. After all, I couldn't half pick 'em: everyone around me seemed to hit the big time! I put my plan to John: we had always been a good team; why not go into the management business together? I even had a first act in mind: in 1968, a singer from New Zealand called John Rowles had hit the UK charts with the song 'If I Only Had Time' following it up with 'Hush, Not A Word To Mary'. To me, he sounded like a cross between Engelbert Humperdinck and Tom Jones, with a little bit of Elvis thrown in. However, John Dee wasn't interested. His only concern was selling his songs to established artistes and then recording them himself.

Then, one evening, a group of us were watching TV at Janie's. Suddenly John Rowles appeared on the screen. John Dee walked in halfway through the first verse, turned to me and said, 'That's the only guy I would sign.'

'Is it?' I replied.

'Yeah, he could be massive. Who is he?'

'John Rowles,' I replied.

'Jesus, you should have put more of a fight! I didn't realise he sang like that. Let's get him!'

Unfortunately we were blocked at every hurdle. Before we approached John Rowles himself, we put out a few feelers to management companies in London, but no one seemed to want to know him. We couldn't understand why – we had the songs and the finance to start recording the next day, Here was a man who, just a year before, had reached number three in the charts!

Then one day John came back from a meeting with a record producer. The producer had told him that Gordon Mills – Tom Jones and Engelbert Humperdinck's manager – had put a block on John Rowles. He said that Gordon saw John as a threat to his acts. I can't confirm if this was true or not, but we didn't want to upset the apple cart, not before John's songs were released for Gordon's company, Valley Music.

Gordon had become a powerful man in the industry – and he wasn't shy about making it known. One afternoon, a few days after the release of 'God Is Love', I ran into him around Janie's. He was seated in the lounge drinking tea. Gordon seemed very distant, acknowledging me only with a '*Mm.*'

Things were getting a little awkward and I was relieved when Janie came into the room. 'Rog is a fellow Welshman, Gordon,' she said. 'He's from your neck of the woods, near Pontypridd. He's got a record out on Deram and it's through your publishing company.' Gordon never even turned to acknowledge her. Eventually he started holding forth on how big Tom and Engelbert had become. 'Bigger than my wildest dreams!' he said. He was looking at Janie, but I had the feeling that he was talking indirectly to me. He kept on and on about how much they were earning, where they were working, about their houses and their Rolls Royce cars.

I stuck it for about half an hour, occasionally butting in with jokes like 'Yes, you can get anything on hire purchase today,' but he never batted an eyelid. He just went on and on about his and Tom's vast wealth, sharing his grand vision of how he was going to take over the music scene of the whole country. Eventually I couldn't stand it any longer and I left. On my way out I remarked, in a not so quiet voice, 'No wonder the English fucking hate us.'

Many years later, when I was working for the United States Air Force as an entertainer, I was based at Hickam Air Force Base which adjoins Pearl Harbour on the island of Oahu, Hawaii. As I was driving through Honolulu one day, I saw John Rowles billed at one of the local nightspots. I was flying out early the next morning so I'm afraid I never got to see him. I learned later that he had returned to live in his native New Zealand. What a shame; I still believe he could have been a huge worldwide star.

John and I soon fell into our old groove, however, working as a duo to secure singers for John's songs, then splitting the profits (still not equally). We were as effective as ever, and soon, to soothe my disappointment over John Rowles, I bought John's Mini. I had to hand it to him: all that work had paid off. It certainly was an eye-catcher. Wherever I drove in London a crowd would gather, wanting to see the inside of the car. Even the police stopped me one night in Edgware Road, just to have a good look at it. I had also acquired, from a friend, a Humber Pullman. It was around fifteen years old but immaculate – as big, if not bigger than, the Rolls Royce Silver Cloud. It was black, had white-walled tyres and a 4149cc engine. If I stopped outside a club someone would rush out to open the door for me – it was that kind of car. Then there was beautiful 1954 Mark VII Jaguar and a very fast souped-up German Ford Taunus. In the meantime, John had acquired a Beach Buggy with a roll bar over the top. In this we drove open-topped through to the Netherlands to negotiate a deal with Fontana Records for a single called 'Gila River' recorded by Cody Smith. It eventually climbed to number five in the pirate radio charts over there.

The cracks were beginning to form between me and Mimi once again. As she was also working we saw less and less of each other. I was still working with my band though, and was now negotiating a record deal for us. Professionally everything seemed fantastic.

It was around about this time that I found out that Janie had a good friend who was a lord. This well-known character apparently liked women to dress up as schoolgirls. He would give them sums to do and scold them if they got them wrong. The more they got wrong, the more he would scold, and that's how he got his kicks. The women were in their twenties and thirties, but if he asked them how old they were, they would have to answer in a childlike voice.

One afternoon Rose mentioned that Janie wanted her to meet the lord. She said Janie had told her that it would be a way to earn some easy money. I said to her that I thought she was only supposed to be working as a housekeeper. She said Janie had been very persuasive but that she still wasn't sure. 'Then don't do it,' I said.

And I assumed she hadn't because, quite frankly, by now she had become completely obsessed with me. She would get upset and throw a tantrum if I went out with John, especially at night, and every visit I made to the house, if I wasn't talking business with John, she would be there by my side. It got to the stage where I started making excuses not to visit the house.

Janie once asked if I would go in to the West End and pick something up for her. It was a package that had been ordered by a very important person, and she had just been preparing to collect it herself, but a friend had telephoned her with a problem and was due to arrive at any minute. I was hesitant at first, but she told me not to make up my mind until I had taken a look outside: there was a car waiting. As I stepped out the front door, I could not believe what I was seeing. The car would have been fit for royalty.

Inside, I sank into the passenger seat, luxuriating in the smell of the leather seating. I asked the chauffeur if he knew our destination. 'Yes,' was his brief reply.

'Drive on then,' I said.

But as we approached the West End, I just couldn't resist. I told the driver to head for Wardour Street. 'That's not our destination,' he protested in a slightly stern voice.

'It is now,' I replied. 'It'll only take a minute or two...' So we headed for Wardour Street and *The Ship*. I got the chauffeur to park in the narrow roadway at the side of the pub and went inside. *The Ship* was busy, as usual. As I entered I recognised two musicians who were standing at the bar. They bought me a drink; they had heard through the grapevine that I had been recording with John and Janie and were eager to learn how we were doing. I asked if they would like to see for themselves, and led them outside. They couldn't believe their eyes. I think they thought I was a pulling a fast one – that is, until I climbed inside and announced, 'Right I'm off now. See you soon. Drive on, Harvey!'

The driver pulled over at our apparent destination, a non-descript premises like so many other shops in London. I had clearly been expected; before the driver had even cut the engine a figure appeared at the front door and ushered me inside. Once the door was closed behind me I was solemnly handed a sealed parcel. No explanation was offered and I didn't hang around to ask for one – the only thing on my mind was that car. Perhaps there would be time for a quick spin around the city before I was expected back?

— CHAPTER TWENTY-ONE —

The Honeycombs

London had changed. Flower power was the big thing and I hated it. It was all love this and love that. If you wore flowers in your hair everything would be fine. It didn't make a blind bit of difference – wars were still going on, people were still killing each other, especially in Vietnam, where more than three million people would die – but still people danced around waving flowers like it would make a difference. Personally, I blamed *The Beatles*, who I had admired tremendously. A couple of years back they had done a photo shoot looking like four pantomime characters: each had grown a moustache, and they were sporting satin, military-style outfits, each a different colour. It had all been downhill from there.

So with Janie and me in tow, John decided that the next step was to conquer America. We would open an office and set up a base in Los Angeles. I had my doubts: it was a big gamble and would take a lot of money – not to mention how our last attempt had turned out! A few days before our planned departure, I received a phone call from Keith Dangerfield (or Keith Ryder as he was now calling himself). He had an appointment the following day with a record producer. The producer was interested in the songs Keith had sent him, and Keith wanted me accompany him to suss if the guy was genuine. I explained to Keith that I would soon be leaving for America and didn't have the time. But he kept on and on, telling me that it could be his big break, how he didn't want to blow it, how he was counting on me. In the end, I reluctantly agreed to go with him.

The following day we ventured out to Buckhurst Hill in Essex. The producer's office was located in Queens Road next to a photographic shop. Upon entering, I was shocked to see that the producer was none other than Martin Murray from *The Honeycombs*! I explained to Keith that Martin and I had played together back in my early days on the London scene; that it was *The Honeycombs* who had put me on to Joe Meek; that without their advice that evening, my career would probably have looked very different. Keith was over the moon. He could see pound signs floating in front of his eyes!

Martin was advertising in the national music papers for singer/songwriters. Those who applied would pay him a fee, I believe around fifty pounds, he would record them and then try to get them a deal with one of the major record labels. Martin certainly had the clout to catch any label's attention: he had been in the music business since the very early '60s, and in 1964 *The Honeycombs's* 'Have I The Right' had gone to number one in the charts in twenty-seven countries. He had eventually left *The Honeycombs*, venturing out as a solo artiste.

Martin was a very agreeable person and, having laid out his plans, left the room to allow me and Keith to discuss our thoughts. I advised Keith that as long as he had a solicitor to look over the contract, he didn't have much to lose. I was just explaining some of Martin's achievements with *The*

Honeycombs when he came back into the room.

'What about *The Honeycombs*!' he exclaimed.

He explained that his old band had gone into hibernation. He had been the leader of *The Honeycombs*, it had been his baby, and it saddened him that they were no longer active and he wanted to keep them alive.

'Join me!' he declared, holding out his hand to me.

'What about me?' Keith cried. But Martin had forgotten all about him. Martin's idea was to put a small orchestra behind the band, to augment the raw rock 'n' roll backing of old, and to develop the vocals. 'A harmony group bigger than *The Beach Boys*!' he enthused. He wanted to concentrate on making big-sounding records, similar to Phil Spector. He told us he had a financier who would put up the money. He wanted me to come back the next morning and meet this person.

I had a big decision to make. It was either America with John and Janie or Essex with Martin. I explained the situation to Martin and he graciously offered me the evening to think things over. But it didn't take me long to make up my mind. I know most people would have picked the glamour of Los Angeles, but Martin's ideas had caught my imagination. It would be an opportunity to step out of John Christian Dee's shadow and become top dog (well, joint top dog with Martin). And anyway, if I didn't like what the financier was offering, and the deal wasn't right, there was still time for me to go to America. I rang Martin later that evening and told him I would meet him the following morning. Keith accompanied me. He was worried that he would not be needed, but I assured him that he would, and should be involved. After all, if it wasn't for him there wouldn't have been a meeting. The financier, whose name was Ron Gibson, turned out to be the owner of the photographic shop situated next door. He had his doubts about the orchestra, but Martin was so persuasive that, in the end, he came round. We would work under the name of *The Honeycombs*, and agreed at first to concentrate on the recording side of things and only after that started to take off to organise a promotion tour. We worked out a percentage deal with Ron, who would finance the recordings and transport, shook hands, and that was that: Martin, Keith and I were *The Honeycombs*.

It was at this time that Mimi and I finally finished. It was all getting too much, we couldn't go on any longer. We were still talking to each other and I visited the children as much as I could. But we saw no future together.

Our job now was to recruit the rest of the band. We decided that we should have two girls. Originally *The Honeycombs* had one girl, the drummer, Ann, or Honey as she was known. Our first audition was with a girl called Maggie. She was from Surrey and had auditioned for Martin before. She had a great harmony voice, was tall and had long black hair – she looked a little bit Spanish. As far as Keith and Martin were concerned, she was in from the moment she first walked in the door!

We recruited a guitarist, previously in the band *Pickettywitch*. Next to be added was a female harmony singer, who also played keyboards. She had also previously auditioned for Martin. We also poached the drummer from Billy J Kramer's band, putting him on a weekly wage. This still didn't seem enough for Martin; a singer/songwriter by the name of Howard Lee was also added. The final piece in the puzzle was a musical director who had previously worked with John Barry and other top arrangers; his job would be to put the orchestra together.

Meanwhile, I was staying with Ron and his wife Ann, Maggie was commuting back and forth from Surrey, Keith was staying with friends in London and the rest of the band were scattered around Essex. After a month or so of rehearsals we were ready to try out the songs with the orchestra. A large hall was hired and the musical director wrote an arrangement for the Peter, Paul, and Mary song 'Leaving On A Jet Plane'. We set up our equipment, marvelled at the number of musicians gathered to perform with us, and waited for the musical director's direction. We were to come in on his cue. Keith would always ask me to sing the first line of his harmony beforehand.

The orchestra started. It was a great sound. The arrangement was beautiful – perhaps too beautiful, because when we were cued to begin, two of the group were too busy listening and came in late. Keith could not get in key and, when he did, he was singing my harmony. Keith often had difficulty pitching; he would always ask me, before a performance, to sing his part to him so he could get in key. Despite this, he had the audacity to say that I had nicked his part! The conductor stopped us and told us to try again and to watch for his cue. Keith was busy '*Mmm Mmmm...*' –ing to himself, trying to work out his harmony. I gave him the note, but by the time the arrangement worked its way round to our cue, he had forgotten it again. The conductor was not impressed, saying that we were not ready to sing with his orchestra and to go away and rehearse. On our way out Ron, who had watched all of this from the side of the venue, turned to me and said, 'I think we should just go with the band and scrub the orchestra.' I agreed.

Around this time, John rang me from Los Angeles. He said that business-wise everything was going well, and that they had set up a company in Ronald Reagan's old offices. On the other hand, his and Janie's relationship had totally broken down. I wasn't especially surprised by this: there had been signs for a while. Janie genuinely liked John's songs and thought, with his talent, he could make a fortune (and that by association, so could she!). However, she had also always maintained that John was a heroin addict – as he had been introduced to her by Long John Baldry. I didn't believe this for a second; to my mind, John's 'addiction' had been a ploy to hook Janie, to get her to take him in the first place. I had known John long before Janie had first met him; we had stayed in hotels together, been out on the town countless times – I'm sure that, over the years, I would have seen some sign of a heroin addiction. John liked his bourbon and cola, but never once did I see him touch anything stronger. But it was incontestable that his behaviour had become erratic, and that the cracks had been showing in his and Janie's relationship for some time. John had become very possessive. I remember once, when we were down in Wiltshire one weekend, his brother-in-law had kept asking Janie to dance. He would not take no for an answer; he was coming on to her. John lost it and hit him in the face.

According to John the breakdown of their relationship was all down to a series of misunderstandings. Janie, however, told me a slightly different story. She said the Mafia had been breathing down John's neck for money; he had owed them for a song writing deal that had backfired, and seeing that one of the Mafia heavies had taken a shine to his diamond ring, had told the man that Tom Jones had given it to him. You could, so John claimed, see Tom wearing it in the introduction to his television show *This is Tom Jones*, the opening shots of which saw Tom grabbing the microphone with the camera zooming in on the ring. He had sold it to the Mafia man for an exorbitant price, but the buyer eventually found out the truth: that it had never belonged to Tom at all. He wanted his money back, with interest. John, of course, couldn't pay and kept fobbing him off, saying that he was expecting a big advance from his Japanese investors. Meanwhile, he had started carrying a gun.

Mixed in with my concern at hearing all of this, I can't deny I felt a little relieved. I was well out of it – or so I thought. Little did I know that John's exploits had someone breathing down *my* neck as well.

— CHAPTER TWENTY-TWO —

Headline News

After our debacle with the orchestra, there was some division within *The Honeycombs*. Martin and I still saw the band solely as a recording unit: we had had a setback, but it was still early days and we could both hear real potential in our sound. However the majority of the band had decided they just wanted to tour and earn some quick cash. Martin conceded and suddenly it was all money, money, money – earn as much as we possibly could! Not only that, but I was to be the de facto band leader while on the road; Martin was adamant that he did not want to tour himself; he would remain in the office and direct proceedings from there. I hadn't signed up for this.

Ron bought a couple of vans and began to concentrate on publicity. He knew many influential business people and was the official photographer to many of the top entertainment venues around London. He was lining up a few gigs for us as well as an audition for a radio series with the BBC at their Maida Vale studios in London. I may have not been too enthused about touring, but they were good opportunities and I saw no point not giving them our all, so we began rehearsing almost daily. That meant most evenings having to drive Maggie to Waterloo Station for her to catch the Guildford train home. As you can imagine, for her this was becoming a bind, so occasionally I would drive her to her parent's home in Weybridge. After a short while, the inevitable happened, and we became an item. This did not go down very well with Keith, as he had been trying to date her too. For a while he was threatening to leave, but he changed his mind a few days later when he met a local Essex girl.

It was after dropping Maggie off at the station one evening that I called into *The Ship* for a drink. I hadn't been there for a while and I wanted to catch up on the West End music scene. As I entered a musician who I had worked with in the past looked up from the bar and caught my eye. He seemed very surprised to see me. 'What are you doing here?' he asked.

'Getting a drink,' I replied.

'Well, be careful.'

He explained that there were some heavies making inquiries about me in the area. Apparently John and I owed them money. I explained to him that I didn't owe anyone any money. 'If John has borrowed money from anyone without my knowledge, then it's his business,' I said. 'It has nothing to do with me.'

'It does if you were spending it together,' he replied.

I asked if he knew who these heavies were, but I couldn't get anything out of him.

'I'd piss off now if I were you,' he advised.

I had to find out who these people were, but how? I couldn't just go from bar to bar asking for someone I didn't know. And I could hardly just sit around waiting until they found me. I had to get back to Essex, buy myself some time, and think things through.

I too was laying low – or trying to anyway; I can't have done to good of a job of it, because one day, for one last time, John phoned me from LA. How he had found out where I was staying, I still don't know. I told him about the heavies and asked what he had borrowed from them. He admitted it was a thousand pounds, but said that he had already paid back five hundred and was going to pay the rest on his return.

'Well, fucking phone them and tell them that!' I shouted. 'They're after me at the moment! I can't go anywhere near the West End!'

'OK, OK,' came the reply. 'I'll phone them now and tell them they'll get the money as soon as I return.' This was the last time that I would speak to him.

I wasn't taking John at his word. It was shit or bust. I decided to head for the club where Jack, the heavy who had fatefully waylaid me from picking up Mimi a couple of years earlier, had introduced me to his villainous acquaintances. If he was there, maybe he could help me. He might be able to check if John had kept his word. Or perhaps he could vouch for me, say that I wasn't involved? At the very least I could ask him for his advice. I left it until late that evening, well after *The Ship* had closed, then I walked nervously to the club. I was taking a big risk; what if Jack wasn't there, but one of the heavies looking for me *was*. I would be serving myself up on a platter. But as I stepped inside, the first person I saw was Jack. I couldn't believe it. The god's must have been with me that night.

'Hi mate, what you been up to?' he asked me. I wondered if I could have a quiet word outside. 'Yeah, sure,' was his reply. I explained everything to him; he told me to wait, out of sight, while he had a word with a few of his associates. I didn't have to wait long; he was back within fifteen minutes. He said that he had made inquiries and the people involved were not currently around. He asked for my home telephone number, which I gave him, and then asked for John's number in Los Angeles. I hesitated. He promised nothing would happen. He said if John had not kept his word and phoned, *he* would phone and give him a gentle reminder.

I have no idea if Jack ever made that call. I imagine that, if he did, he would have struggled to get through, because Janie and John's line must have been ringing off the hook. In February 1971 *The News of the World* ran a big story with the headline 'SEX AND CASH PAYOLA FOR TV PRODUCER'. Someone at President Records, the company that had released Janie's last single, 'Back On My Feet Again', had had a meeting with some music executives. Or at least, so he had thought – the music executives were in reality undercover reporters. There, the President Records man had let slip that it was possible to bribe DJs to play records, all but guaranteeing the song's success. He had gone on to mention Janie's parties. The two reporters, maintaining their cover as music executives, had infiltrated one of these parties. With that the wave of accusations against Janie reached the nation's – and my – attention.

Janie, the article alleged, had been a madam at the centre of an extensive prostitution ring; not only this, but she had been offering her prostitutes' services to BBC agents for free as a reward for playing records. I couldn't believe it! This was followed up, in June 1971, with another sensational article, about Janie's involvement in a call-girl ring and the scandal at the BBC. Janie was in serious trouble.

It was around this time I started seeing a bit more of my children. I felt I had been missing out on so much. Most of it was my fault, but I needed to see them. My son, Cary, was now six and Sasha, my daughter, four. I wanted to take them both to my parents' house in Wales. My mother and father last saw them when they came to London when I had meningitis. Cary would have been three then and Sasha one year old. Unfortunately, Sasha was unable to come with us. She wasn't very well at the time, so I ended up just taking Cary. He was a lovely good natured little child, very handsome with jet black hair, and everyone adored him. We spent our time visiting relatives and climbing a few mountains. I don't believe he had ever seen a mountain before.

At the time, I wasn't sure how he would take being away from home with me. Let's face it, he hadn't seen much of me in the past few years, but he seemed happy enough and he enjoyed himself. Everywhere he went he was being made a fuss of.

By the time we returned to London Sasha had recovered from her illness. I took her out for the day to the Serpentine in Hyde Park and then on to Regents Park, where I was going to take her to the zoo. I don't think she liked the zoo much, she didn't want to go in. If she didn't want to go in, there was no way I could make her. She was a lovely, beautiful little girl, lighter hair than Cary, but a little more fiery when she wanted to be.

*

Before our audition with the BBC, we were to play a few nights on the nightclub circuit in south Wales. We were hoping this would get us up to speed before what would be a real opportunity for us: if the audition went well, we would be recording a six-week radio series for the BBC called *Here Come The Honeycombs* (although we were to change that to *The New Honeycombs*).

Responsibility for running the tour had been subcontracted to Cardiff agent Don Tyror. I was to contact Don when we reached the first venue of the tour – a big club in Cwmbran – to find out what accommodation he had booked for us. But on our arrival, in my excitement about what was for me, of course, a homecoming tour, I completely forgot. Howard reminded me in the interval, and I went out to the foyer to use the payphone. There was so much noise in the club that I could barely hear the phone ringing his end, and when he did answer I had to shout. I told him who I was and that I was ringing to find out the address of the accommodation. He began to tell me the address and how to get there, but I had to ask him to start again. 'Pardon, could you repeat that? There's so much noise in here.' Out of nowhere, he went into a rage, shouting down the line, calling me a fucking so and so, ranting and raving like a lunatic. In the end I slammed the receiver down.

I went back and told the rest of the band that the man was a crank, suggesting that we should book into a hotel and use his commission to pay part of the bill. Keith, however, argued that he would try ringing him when the noise had quietened down a bit, which he did. When he came back to the dressing room, I asked Keith if the nutter had flown off the handle again, and he replied, 'No, he was as nice as pie.'

The accommodation, or digs as we would call it, was in Ruthin Gardens, Cardiff, and was run by a Mrs Jones. In future it would become well-known in the world of show business. The actor Leonard Rossiter was once asked on a TV chat show what it was like for him in the early days performing in theatres around the country. He was asked if he had stayed in hotels or theatrical digs. He replied that he stayed in digs, as he couldn't afford hotels. The host then asked what were the worst digs he had ever stayed in, and without hesitation, he replied 'Ruthin Gardens in Cardiff.'

Mrs Jones, as I remember, was a short, plump woman, slow and very stern. On our first morning there, she appeared from the kitchen asking if we would like cereal or fried breakfast. We assumed she meant cereal first. But we were wrong: if you chose the cereal, you wouldn't get the fried breakfast.

Then there was the no smoking rule. It wasn't just that you weren't allowed to smoke in the house: you weren't allowed to anywhere outside either. Mrs Jones would be on smoking watch throughout the day. When she entered the room, she'd be sniffing as she walked along, saying that she could smell tobacco smoke. And if you were stood outside for whatever reason, the blinds would twitch as she kept an eye on you. Nearly everyone smoked in those days and this was like being back in school. But it could have been worse: years later I was talking to one of the musicians from *Dave Dee, Dozy, Beaky, Mick and Tich*, and he told me that when a couple of them had stayed there, Mrs Jones had had them shelling peas for her.

The sign outside promised: 'Bed, breakfast and evening meal'. I'm still waiting for my breakfast! Needless to say, we didn't stay long.

Luckily, Don Tyror seemed to have completely changed; I don't know if he was feeling guilty or if he was worried about his commission, but either way, he rang and asked if we would like to stay at his home in Cathedral Road, Cardiff, for the duration of the tour. I was a little sceptical, thinking back to that phone call, but everyone else jumped at the offer.

When we arrived at Don's we were greeted by his wife, Betty, a lovely lady, who showed us to our rooms. That night's gig in Pontypridd went well; Don and his sidekick Monty were there to watch our show, and they seemed impressed – all in all, everything was running smoothly. That is, until breakfast the next morning. As we sat chatting around the table, an electrician, who Betty had called in to repair some of the lights, asked her a question. Don answered, but it was difficult to understand him as he had his mouth full. 'Pardon,' the electrician said and that was it. Don went off on one, effing and blinding, as we looked on in amazement. The electrician took his ladder down and left, and as if a switch had been flipped, Don resumed chatting as if nothing happened. Betty had a word with us later, telling us that she had forgotten to give him his medication. If Don wouldn't take it, she would have to slip it into his tea.

That night we were awoken by an almighty hammering sound. We all simultaneously ran out of our rooms to the landing. Looking over the banister we saw Don with an axe in his hand, trying to chop down the door to one of the downstairs rooms – a room which a nurse from the local hospital had rented. We found out later that she had gone for a drink with Betty, while Don had been out at some club. Betty eventually calmed the situation down and after much persuasion, Don retired to his bedroom. The following morning he was as right as rain again. We had two more nights to stay at Don's and some of the band wanted to find other digs, but Betty convinced them everything would be OK.

The following evening we were doing the double – playing two clubs in one evening. The late venue was *The Casablanca Club* in Mount Stuart Square, Tiger Bay. I remember Big Les on the door: he carried most of our equipment in for us on his own. And you could see why they had hired him, because Tiger Bay hadn't changed a bit. Les told me that recently a girl had one of her breasts cut off in the club by a merchant seaman.

It was a good night for us; everything seemed to gel. After the show Don walked into the dressing room, congratulated us on a great performance and announced that he had some good news and some bad news for us.

Keith said, 'Go on then, Don, give us the good news.'

'They liked you,' Don replied, referring to the club management and audience.

'Great, what's the bad news?'

'They want you to play the rest of the week here', said Don.

I chipped in and said that we couldn't do it. Don was contracted to get us our early spots, but our late spots were the responsibility of George Beynon. We had only worked *The Casablanca* as it had been our evening off, but what Don was now suggesting would involve us cancelling all of our late evening bookings. George owned many top nightspots throughout south Wales and there was no way I was going to cross him. Don eventually relented, agreeing that it would be in his interest to keep in with George.

But that night, as Maggie and I we were in bed asleep, Don and Monty appeared at our bedroom door. They were very drunk. They wanted Maggie to follow them downstairs for a drink. They kept telling her that they could make her a star.

She replied, 'But I am a star.'

'Now fuck off,' I added, which they did.

Things came to a head the next day when Don called me, Maggie and Keith into his office. He had booked us an early evening spot, which he was well within his rights to do, but the venue was far too close to our late venue, one of George Beynon's clubs. As we explained, our contract with George Beynon stated that we could not play within a certain radius of one of his nightclubs. Don insisted.

'No way,' I declared.

'OK,' replied Don. 'I'll get Monty up here to sort you out.'

'Get who the hell you like, we're not doing it!' So we waited until it became clear that Monty wasn't turning up. Undaunted, Don declared, 'I'm going to phone Micky and Wicky. They'll sort you out for good. You'll be sorry for this!'

Micky and Wicky – those were names that I hadn't heard in a long time. Everyone from my neck of the woods knew Micky and Wicky. They were two lads from the village where I was born, sort of like the local Kray twins.

They knew my grandmother and treated her with the utmost respect. Don't get me wrong, they were hard nuts and you never wanted to anger them, but I wasn't worried in the slightest. I leaned over to Maggie and remarked, making sure Don could hear me, 'I haven't seen Micky and Wicky for years!' This seemed to do the trick, as Don put down the phone in surprise. 'It's the only venue I've got for you,' he said, changing tack.

After much soul searching John, the guitarist, came up with an idea. 'What if we do it in disguise?'

In the end, we didn't quite go so extreme as to disguise ourselves. We just went in jeans and T-shirts and played under the name *Rigor Mortis And The Gravediggers*. Interestingly the venue asked to re-book us. Don said we could always come back and do a tour under that name if everything fell through with our current projects.

Although I would hardly have believed it then, I did actually take him up on his offer – well not staging a comeback with *Rigor Mortis and the Gravediggers*, but returning for a tour. In fact I kept in contact with Don for many years; whenever I needed work, Don was there for me, and he became a friend as well as an agent. I heard a story about him once, a few year later, on one of my visits back to Wales. According to one of the local musicians, *The Casablanca Club* had decided to put on a few rock 'n' roll nights. Apparently, one of their acts had been Marty Wilde. Marty had arrived late afternoon with his band *The Wildcats* and they had spent a while in the club chatting to the organiser and staff.

Upon returning to the van, however, they found it had been broken into and most of the equipment stolen. After returning to the club and calling the police, they ventured outside once again to find that the van had been nicked as well! The police weren't at all helpful, so someone from the club phoned Don Tyror to ask for his help. Within three hours the band received a call telling them where they could pick up their equipment and van. Don to the rescue!

We completed a successful run in south Wales, but already the cracks were forming in the band. Our keyboard-player's fiancé was becoming jealous of our success. With the thought of a radio series looming, and the talk of television appearances, he began putting pressure on her to leave. On our return to London, she did exactly that. I wanted to replace her; she had added a lot to our sound. But the rest of the band wanted to carry on without her. Obviously – they would get more money this way! I switched from bass to rhythm guitar to cover the gaps she had left in our sound, and took over lead vocals. I assumed that we would recruit another bass player, but everyone, excluding Maggie, was adamant that we didn't need one. They wanted me to switch to bass when needed. In fact, Keith stated that we could get by without any instruments at all that we could become an a cappella band!

So in our depleted state, we auditioned for the radio series at the BBC studios in Maida Vale. While we waited for their decision, I lobbied hard for the hiring of some more musicians, but the group was adamant – moreover, they wanted to make the most of their newly increased earnings, so insisted we tour. We managed to book a tour of the North, playing most of the top nightspots and appearing with many of the day's big stars. It was hard work but personally I enjoyed it. That is, except for the week at the cabaret spot *The Kingsway Club* in Southport. We were required to do our performance while the punters polished off their meals. There was not much applause that week. The audience were not going to put down their cutlery after every song just to clap. We found out that Freddie Starr would be appearing there the following week, so we left word with the resident band to warn Freddie what to expect.

I discovered that, when he did appear, Freddie had, halfway through a number, stepped onto the tables, stamping his way along, smashing the crockery underfoot. There were steaks flying everywhere! He then casually walked back, still on the table tops, and to the stage, finished the song and said, 'Good evening, ladies and gentlemen, nice to be here'.

Howard Lee hated every minute of touring. Every city we played, he tried to get a doctor's note to say he was too ill to carry on. All he wanted to do was get back home to his girlfriend. The touring life was not for him. The other boys would take the piss out of him because he would wear flowered pyjamas to bed, with a toothbrush sticking out of his pyjama coat pocket. He would be constantly on the phone to his girlfriend complaining about how we were mistreating him. Predictably, after the tour finished he was gone. We were now two people short, and except for Maggie and me, the rest of the band still did not want any replacements – it was suicidal starting a radio show as we were. I tried to persuade Martin to re-join us just for the series but he refused. He was happy in the office. It was then that we received word from the BBC that there was a possibility of a one-off show but not a series. I was oddly relieved. But by now, there was so much bickering going on that I had decided enough was enough. I told everyone that I would fulfil any remaining engagements, then leave. Ray, the drummer, said if I was going, then so was he. Maggie and John, the lead guitarist, followed. I asked Keith what he was going to do. He said that he hadn't decided, but maybe, if possible, with Martin's consent he would recruit new members and continue working as either *The Honeycombs* or *The New Honeycombs*. I did hear later that he reformed the band and did a tour of America, but I never saw him again.

On their return to England, Janie and John decided to get a divorce. John moved out and into a flat, which Janie said she had financed, but not before they received a visit from the Mafia. Luckily for John, a friend of Janie's paid off the debt. He must have also paid the London heavies as one day I had a phone call from Jack to say everything had been settled. He told me that he was finishing with all that type of work and going straight. Funnily enough, he had met a young lady in *The Ship*. They were moving in together and had purchased a house in North London. I thanked him and wished him all the best for the future.

When John again ran out of money, however, Janie alleged that he started threatening her and some of her friends. According to her she was at the stage where she was afraid to venture outdoors. Apparently John would sit in his car outside her house all night, threatening her visitors.

But Janie and John had bigger problems than each other. The police, who had been following up on *The News Of The World*'s claims, had also been investigating the lord. While Janie had still been in America, he had offered her £10,000 to come home and help him fight the case, which she accepted. But when the case reached the courts and the lord was called to give evidence, to protect himself he told them that Janie had been blackmailing him – that she had demanded the £10,000. He really laid it on thick, telling the court of his heart condition, how he had almost died... This was all reported in the press. He was asked if Janie's actions had adversely affected him. 'Very much so,' he replied. In spite of all this Janie was cleared of all blackmail charges.

For the time being anyway. A fresh set of charges materialised and a new trial was held at the Old Bailey in January 1973. Janie was acquitted on the payola charges, but was jailed for seven years for operating a call-girl service. The judge remarked that she had lured girls into a web of vice by false promises to get them work in television and films. Once they realised what they had let themselves in for, he said, she prevented their escape by threatening to expose them to their parents or employers. The judge summed up: 'In my time, I have come across many men whom it would be right to describe as evil, but in all my time at the Bar and on the Bench, I have only come across one woman, so far as I can recall, who merited such a comparison. You are the second, and beside you, she was comparatively harmless.'

John, who had been implicated in many of the charges, was cleared of all wrongdoing. I was long out of touch with him at this stage, and followed the case through the papers. My daughter, Sasha, did happen to bump into John in the late '80s in a pub near Swiss Cottage, but that was the first and last contact anyone I know has had with him since the case. I did manage to find out on the Internet that, after being cleared, John left the country and returned to Germany, where he was later jailed for stabbing his girlfriend. He escaped and disappeared somewhere in France. Knowing John as I did, he probably changed his name, learned the language and blended into the recording industry there. Reports also suggest that he died in London in 2004, but other reports say 2002 and 2006.

— CHAPTER TWENTY-THREE —

Ddraig Recording Studios

After the band split, Maggie and I decided to head for south Wales. We had made a considerable amount of contacts in the area, and were hoping to try our luck as a double act.

Before leaving I visited the children and explained that I would be touring the country but I would keep in touch. I'm not sure if they totally understood what I was telling them; they were still quite young.

South Wales, just like the north east of England, had a large, vibrant club circuit, and by the end of our first week back we already had played two clubs in Cardiff. In one, we met Jake, a musician who had recently set up his own recording studio. The studio was called Ddraig (Welsh for dragon) and was located in Canton. Jake was looking for someone with London contacts to procure recording contracts for his list of bands and singers, and thought we might be a good fit. He invited us to visit the studio the next day for a chat.

As we entered the studio the following day, we were met by Jake, Carl Leighton-Pope and Dai Shell. The three of them had set up Ddraig together. Carl had been born in the mining village of Gifach Goch – a place I knew well – but was now running a car hire business in London. In the future Carl would go on to run his own international booking agency, representing such acts as Michael Buble, Bryan Adams, Mica Paris, Billy Ocean, Bonnie Tyler, Van Morrison and many more. Dai Shell would go on to form the band *Sassafras*, which Carl would manage, but for now they were all struggling for money.

We agreed to work together. They would find the best bands and singer songwriters in Wales and record them; I would negotiate a recording deal for them in London. Initially there were three acts that interested us: a singer called Laverne Brown (a great smooth soul voice), Mickey Gee (the resident guitarist at *The Casablanca Club* and the lead guitarist in Tom Jones's first band), and Shakin' Stevens (or Shaky as he was called). Shaky had been around on the rock 'n' roll circuit for a while. At the time he was managed by a guy from Penarth named Mike Barratt, which coincidentally was also Shaky's real name.

We recorded six tracks with Shaky, country rock numbers such as 'White Lightning', the old George Jones' song. He was very quiet and hardly ever spoke; it was a struggle getting through to him at times. Voice and recording wise, though, I couldn't fault him; each song would be finished in a couple of takes. As I saw it, there didn't seem much chance of Mike Barratt getting a deal for Shaky, so, we persuaded Mike to sign him over to us on a temporary contract – if we couldn't obtain a recording deal for him, then our contract would be null and void.

Laverne, too, was a pleasure to work with. He had a great voice, like a cross between Sam Cooke and Richie Havens.

Mickey, on the other hand, was a bit temperamental; he

was an excellent guitarist, and would in the 1980s play on many of Shakin' Stevens hit records. For now, however, he was skint – and tetchy about it.

One morning, while speaking to a contact of mine in London, I learned that *Manfred Mann* were looking for a guitarist. I immediately thought that this would be a great opportunity for Mickey. He would be playing with a top band, with the chance to get some of his songs recorded. I suggested to Mickey to try out for the job. At first, he seemed very reluctant to do so. I couldn't understand why he was so unenthusiastic. He certainly needed the money, and I had great faith in him as a musician.

After much persuasion, I eventually managed to talk him round, and I arranged an audition for him at a venue in Tottenham Court Road.

He left the following morning, full of enthusiasm, and was back by late evening. I asked him how everything had gone. Had he passed the audition?

'Yes,' he replied.

'Great!' I said. 'When do you start?'

'I'm not.'

'What do you mean you're not? Why not?'

'Because they're fucking crap!' he announced.

So that was that: Mickey refused the job with *Manfred Mann* – a job that would have got him out of a hole, and not only that, he would have the prestige of playing with a named band – who knows, they might have recorded a few of his songs? But that was Mickey: unpredictable.

I took Mickey's songs to Frank Rodgers at Decca. Frank was the brother of the singer Clodagh Rodgers, who had had a few hit records in 1969 and represented the UK in the

1971 Eurovision Song Contest. Frank liked the songs and tried valiantly to get a recording deal for Mickey, but ultimately failed. Mickey had the talent, and his songs were very good, but I think his temperament didn't help him. He had developed a reputation, and people were afraid to take a chance on him. Meanwhile, I took Laverne's demo songs to United Artists. They said that Laverne had a great voice but he sounded *too* much like Richie Havens. But they liked the sound that was being produced at Ddraig. I couldn't believe my ears when they said that they would like to visit the studio to see the set up. So, between us, we arranged a date for the visit.

This was a first: a huge organisation like United Artists wanting to visit a small recording studio (which had once been a local shop) in Wales. Reading between the lines, I think they had wanted to replicate the success of Rockfield Studios near Monmouth (which in 1973 would host the recording sessions for Queen's *Bohemian Rhapsody*).

On the day of their visit there was great excitement in the building. Everything had been set up to run smoothly, including which songs we were going to play. When they arrived, we were drinking coffee in the studio and everything was calm. That is, until Mickey entered the premises, stomping around the small office, hounding me. I took him aside and tried to calm him down – his timing couldn't have been worse: Dai had just started playing the executives some of our most recent recordings. After an hour and a half, the executives finally emerged from the studio, only to find Mickey still badgering me. He was shouting that he wanted two grand up front – I'm not even sure what for! I don't know what he was on, but whatever it was, it wasn't doing our cause any good. In the end, Maggie told him to shut up and he did – she'd always had his number. The two executives left with the promise that they would be in touch. Despite Mickey, we had high hopes; they seemed so positive and had been knocked out by the sound of the recordings Dai had played them. They were even talking about the possibility of relocating the studio to bigger premises, with accommodation and better parking facilities. I tried my hardest to get a deal in London for Shaky. EMI told me that there was no room for his kind of music anymore – it was old and dated. Decca came to the same conclusion. I bet they were all eating their hats when Shaky became the biggest selling recording artiste of the '80s. It wasn't until 1977, when Shaky was playing a gig in London, that he was spotted by television producer Jack Good, who invited him to attend an audition in London for a part in the *Elvis* musical. Shaky played Elvis in his army and movie years, with, I believe, Tim Whitnall as the young Elvis and PJ Proby portraying his Vegas phase. From there, for Shaky it was a one way street to stardom, though much too late for me of course: as stipulated, our contract was nullified when we were unable to secure him a recording deal.

In the meantime Maggie and I still had to earn money ourselves. Maggie had managed to negotiate a short tour of the north east, and had booked us accommodation at Jesmond House in Page Bank, Spennymoor, Co Durham. Jesmond House, better known as 'The Farm' to the bands and entertainers of the time, was a converted old school that had been bought by one of its former pupils, a man called Peter. He and his wife, Rita, had converted it into theatrical digs. Many famous pop groups, singers, duos and comedians stayed there. It was a sprawling old building, with around seven bedrooms and just one bathroom. Often there would be over twenty-five people staying there, and the bands would sleep four to a room. The back door would always be left open for those returning late at night, and there were no locks on the bedroom doors. Some singers would arrive in their own caravans. Rita and Peter would allow them to stay in the grounds for a small fee and have their breakfast and early-evening meal in the main house. Rita and Peter were a lovely couple, and Rita became like a second Mum to all the acts.

Wherever we travelled, we would always try and take in the local sights. One afternoon, we stopped for a coffee at a café in the small town of Shildon. The café was empty, apart from a girl behind the counter, whose name was Theresa. After general chit chat, she informed us that there was a small nightclub above the café, that it had just opened, and that it was owned by her fiancé George Reynolds. She said we should call in one evening, as they had late entertainment most nights.

After finishing our drinks, we thanked her and said that we would call in again soon. It would be sooner than we thought. The next day, the agency we were working for rang to ask if we would like to do a late spot at a small nightclub nearby. It turned out to be the little club above the café.

On the day of our gig we waited backstage for what seemed like an age. Eventually there was a knock at the door, and a man dressed in a black suit, white shirt and black bow tie entered. I ordered a pint of lager and a glass of lime and soda for Maggie.

'Right, sir,' he replied.

'And,' I added before he could leave, 'could you please tell the manager to get himself in here and let us know what time we're on, or we'll be off!'

'Very good, sir', came the reply. Within a couple of minutes, he was back with the drinks. I asked if he had told the manager.

'No need, sir, I am the owner,' he replied. He held out his hand. 'George Reynolds,' Of course! George Reynolds – hence the name of the venue: *The GR Club*. I had been mouthing off to the owner, who I found out later had been an ex-street fighter and professional safe blower! He had started his crime spree in the sixties, working in London with some well-known criminal gangs. He ended up doing a stretch in prison and, after his release, George had managed to acquire enough money to open the café and club. We never asked just where he had 'acquired' the money.

We had a very good reception from the audience and, after we had finished our spot, George brought a few drinks to the dressing room. He told us that we were a great act and he thought we could really go places. Maggie replied we already had, but it had been a nightmare. We both got on really well with George; he was a character all right. We didn't leave the club until the early hours of the morning. As we left he told us that if we ever needed anything doing, he could do it, and if we needed a manager anytime he was the man for the job. We told him about the studio in Wales, but said that if it didn't work out, we would be back up the north east to take up his offer.

Back in Cardiff, we tried everything to make the studio work, but, having never heard back from United Artists, and with our artists struggling to obtain recording contracts, it seemed doomed to failure. We released Shaky from his contract, and Maggie and I considered whether to return to Weybridge, continue working Wales, or to venture back to the north east and work with George.

— CHAPTER TWENTY-FOUR —

The North East

We took up George's offer. With his contacts he became our lifeline, and it wasn't long before he introduced us to an agent, Trevor Shaw, and we were working seven nights a week (an early and late spot, plus some afternoon shows). We were now averaging a minimum of fourteen shows a week. At first, we lived in a rented house in Shildon, but as time went on we moved back into Jesmond House in Spennymoor, County Durham, where there was a fresh set of fellow performers: *Hot Chocolate*, *The Sweet*, *Smokey*, *The Casuals* and many more. It was hard work in the north east, but we were enjoying really earning our crust.

But I must admit I was missing London and would visit at every opportunity, to see the children and roam around my old West End haunts. On one occasion, whilst sitting and drinking a coffee in the *The Gioconda* in walked a face from the past – a singer/songwriter who played guitar and went by the name of Russ Hamilton. I had not known Russ in his heyday, but had seen him around London now and again in the mid-60s. Russ had a huge hit in the UK in 1957 with 'We Will Make Love', while the B-side, 'Rainbow', reached number four in the US charts, both self-penned. Russ's own career was practically over by the early '60s, but he did keep writing for other people. He approached me from across the café and said that he knew my face. We sat drinking coffee and reminiscing. Although I had never known Russ, it was great meeting someone who'd known the London I knew: the London of the '50s and '60s. I enjoyed every minute of our chat. I believe that Russ was the first successful British singer/songwriter to gain hits both here and America. We said our goodbyes and I was off to see the kids and take them out, before returning back up north.

Many of the '50s and '60s bands and singers who had been packing out the London coffee houses just a few years previously were now on the northern club circuit. One such figure was the American Johnny Duncan, who had had a huge hit in 1957 with the song 'Last Train To San Fernando'. Another was Karl Denver, in the charts in 1961 with 'Wimoweh'. Then there was Emile Ford, now working on his own, but who earlier, with his band *The Checkmates*, had had a number one with 'What Do You Want to Make Those Eyes At Me For'. Also, Billy J Kramer, now without *The Dakotas*. We worked with them all, with me reminiscing with Billy J about the times in *The Cavern*.

As well as the solo singers, most of the '60s bands played the northern circuit. *Gerry and the Pacemakers*, *The Merseys*, *The Fortunes*, *The Nashville Teens* (one of *The Nashville Teens* had actually worked for Maggie's father) and there were many, many more.

George, unfortunately, got himself into trouble again over some stolen guitars and was locked away in Gloucester. This time it had been a mistake on the police's part and he was soon released. He brought in a few songwriters to write some material for us, but the songs were not strong enough.

As well as working the north east we were now touring Scotland and Wales. George was gradually building up his empire, and music was only part of it. He was into everything: recovering the seating in working men's clubs, supplying kitchen worktops... He would soon become super rich, appearing in *The Times* rich list and buying and selling Darlington Football Club. Unfortunately, as George became more successful, things deteriorated between Maggie and me. The constant travelling and the amount of work we were doing – she just couldn't sustain it. We were booked up constantly for at least a year ahead, including two shows on Christmas Day! The money was great – we were on top in that respect – and Maggie was saving hers, but everything I earned was going towards paying off my debts. I ended up with virtually nothing in my pocket at the end of the week. I didn't know how long we could keep going with the continual workload and constant travelling. In the end it just got too much for Maggie and she packed what she could carry, heading back to her parents' home. She appeared to be having a minor breakdown, but it was worse than I thought; she ended up for a short time in a sanatorium.

I carried on for a while as a solo singer, but in my newfound loneliness, I had started getting drunk most nights. I was even drunk a few times on stage. My work was deteriorating and it was my own fault – worse, it was getting back to the agents. My workload began to drop from seven nights a week down to just two or sometimes three. I was living in a large caravan at the back of Jesmond House. I knew most of the bands that stayed at the main house and, after they finished their gigs, they would end up in the caravan with me, either playing guitar or listening to music, but always drinking until daylight. The less work I got, the more I drank. I was on a downward spiral, and then the depression started to kick in.

Then, unexpectedly, I was offered a tour with Bobby Thompson. Bobby Thompson, nicknamed 'The Little Waster', was a comedian – a legend and an institution in the north east. When I first saw him perform, at the *Variety Club* in Spennymoor, I could hardly understand a word he said – his Geordie accent was that thick. I don't believe he ever worked further south than Doncaster. It was great fun working with Bobby: the clubs would be packed every night, and I was back on top form. Only one thing annoyed me. I would open the show and do a thirty to forty-minute warm up spot, Bobby would then do the main middle spot, and I would finish the evening off with another thirty or forty minutes. As it was Bobby's show, he would be paid the fee for the gig as he came off stage. He would then, just before I finished my second spot, with people still on the floor dancing, walk up to the stage, lift one of the heavy microphone stand legs, and place my fee underneath it, in view of everyone. Every night I would ask him to leave it with the concert secretary, but he would always reply: 'It's safer under there, bonnie lad.'

Before long the tour had finished and, with the money burning a hole in my pocket, things gradually went back to the way they had been. I would be working Saturday and Sunday evenings, if I was lucky, getting a Friday night to go with it, and the rest of the time I would be drunk.

One sozzled evening, I thought of returning to London. But

deep down I knew there was nothing left there for me. The scene had changed, the faces had changed. Who would I know there now? How would I get work? I would have to start all over. I couldn't go through that again. But then again, if I stayed in the north east, what would I do? My work in the clubs was declining. I was earning money but only just enough to survive on. There was only one thing for it, I thought. Then suddenly, there was a loud knock on the caravan door, then another. I swung open the door, and there stood Freddy, a singer from one of the bands staying in Jesmond House at the time – a successful outfit that had just started to make it in the recording industry. I thought I had seen him for the last time a month or so earlier, after a late-night drinking session, as they had just been about to go on tour. But as he entered the caravan, he explained that he and the band had thought that they might as well as earn some extra money up here for a few nights. I was glad to see him again. When we had first met, he would always want to know what it was like in the '50s and '60s, who had I worked with, the people I had known. He was fascinated that I had actually been involved in the music scene in the '50s and would eagerly want to know what went on. He would always be picking my brain about the recording business. He had only ever played in the workingmen's clubs, but a top management company was interested in him, and he had wanted as much information as I could give him. But now he was the one giving me advice: how I had to get out, get out of my rut, maybe go back to Wales for a while to clear my head. He told me I still had a lot of talent, and with a clear head and a new environment, I would see things differently. We talked through the night and I slept through the next day.

A day later, I told Rita and Peter, the couple who owned Jesmond House, that I was leaving for good. I left everything behind except my clothes and my musical equipment. I had phoned earlier to ask my parents if it would be OK to return home, and they said they would be delighted to see me.

I took the scenic route home. I still didn't really know what I wanted to do. Did I honestly want to go back to Wales? I would probably end up working in a factory or driving a wagon. But Freddy was right: I had to get out of it, out of the north east, out of the music scene – I had to get my head together. I drove slowly, stopping often. Eventually I pulled in at the side of a railway bridge, stopped the engine and lay back in my seat to think things through. Every so often I could hear the sound of the trains as they passed underneath me. Maybe I should leave the car and equipment and catch a train somewhere? Then I looked out of the window and saw a telephone box. I stepped out of the car, walked to the telephone box, picked up the phone and dialled a number. The phone rang and rang, and I was just about to hang up when there was a click and a voice on the other end said, 'Hello.'

'Hi Sas.'

'Daddy, when are you coming to see us?'

'Soon,' I said. 'Very soon. I'm going back to Wales for a while, but then I'll come and see you.'

'All right, Daddy.'

Suddenly I knew exactly what to do. I headed for the car, took my guitar case out of the boot, walked along to the middle of the bridge and I laid it on the floor. I opened the case and took out my old Gretsch guitar. To the whistle of an approaching train, I looked at it for the last time. Then I flung it as far as I could, on to the railway line. It landed on its body with the neck sticking up. Before it had chance to fall flat the train ploughed into it, smashing it to pieces. I got back in my car and drove off, a wave of relief flowing over me. It felt as if though I'd thrown all my troubles away.

— EPILOGUE —

'You'll be on in about two minutes, Rog. The singer's nearly finished his last number.'

Those words startled me. I was daydreaming and hadn't heard the compère knock the door and enter.

'Oh, Oh, OK,' I replied. I picked up my glass and took a swig. My mind started racing. Would I remember the words? They were my songs but I still had a job remembering them. Would I remember the chord structure? And be able to see the fret...

Too late I was on.

I heard the compère announcing me and I stepped onto the stage...

Then & Now

Available from Candy Jar Books

DR STRANGELOVE: OR HOW I LEARNED TO STOP WORRYING AND LOVE THE BOMB
by Peter George

It is the height of the Cold War and the two power-blocs stand on the brink of war. On a routine patrol, US bombers receive a coded message. Doomsday has arrived; the fight for democracy, freedom and bodily fluids has just gone nuclear…

The official novelisation of the classic film, Dr Strangelove or: How I Learned to Stop Worrying and Love the Bomb is a hilarious and provocative satire of the madness of Mutually Assured Destruction. Featuring impotent generals, a sieg-heiling scientist and one very Big Board, this is how the world ends, not with a whimper, but enough megatonnage to make you abandon monogamy.

Written by Peter George, co-screenwriter of the film and author of Two Hours to Doom, the novel that inspired it, this brand-new edition also features a foreword by David George and the never-before-published 'Strangelove's Theory', a short story on the mastermind as a younger man.

Based on Stanley Kubrick's film Dr Strangelove. Screenplay by Stanley Kubrick, Peter George and Terry Southern.

ISBN: 978-0-9931191-4-9

Also available from Candy Jar Books

LETHBRIDGE-STEWART: THE FORGOTTEN SON
by Andy Frankham-Allen

For Colonel Alistair Lethbridge-Stewart his life in the Scots Guards was straightforward enough; rising in the ranks through nineteen years of military service. But then his regiment was assigned to help combat the Yeti incursion in London, the robotic soldiers of an alien entity known as the Great Intelligence. For Lethbridge-Stewart, life would never be the same again.

Meanwhile in the small Cornish village of Bledoe a man is haunted by the memory of an accident thirty years old. The Hollow Man of Remington Manor seems to have woken once more. And in Coleshill, Buckinghamshire, Mary Gore is plagued by the voice of a small boy, calling her home.

What connects these strange events to the recent Yeti incursion, and just what has it all to do with Lethbridge-Stewart?

"A solid start to the series. The Brigadier is such an integral part of Doctor Who mythos, it seems right and proper he now has his own series." – Doctor Who Magazine

ISBN: 978-0-9931191-5-6